I GIVE MY EYES...

stories + conversations + dreams

it happens, it shows itself, a rim of red on the horizon cloud,

then the first hint of fire, until finally, oh yes, there it is, there it is.

An unbroken thread of sunlight stretching halfway around the

world, flowing back to the endless islands of landless algae floating

in primordial seas, algae that turned and twisted and crunched up

and congealed into us, you and me, vast conglomerations

of cellular flesh desperately searching for water and light

and air and earth and a place to live and die."

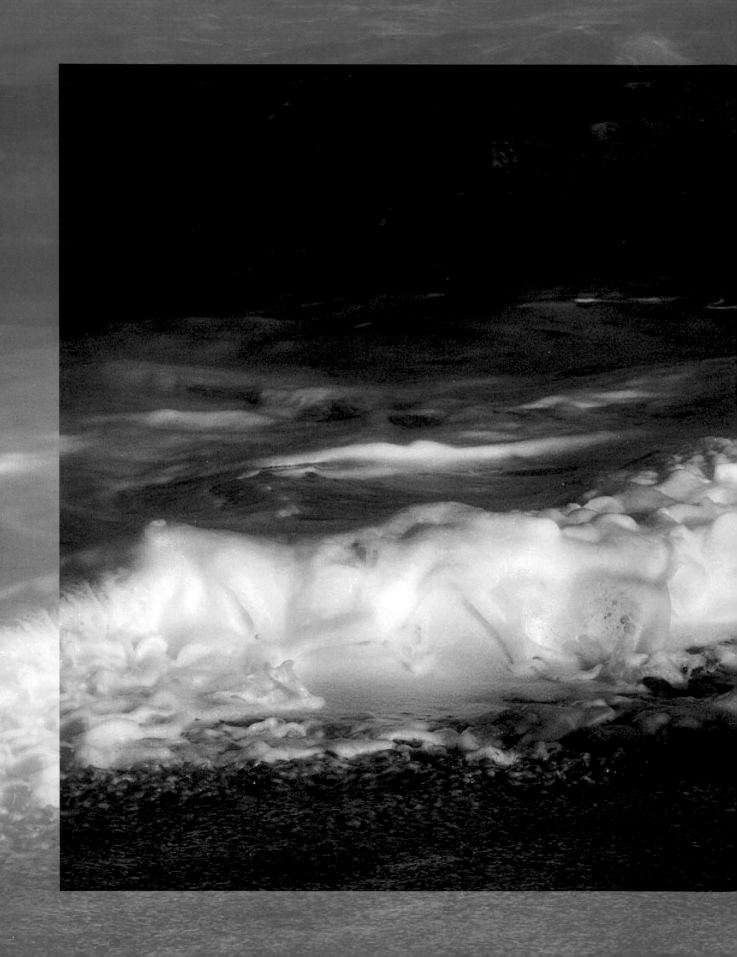

"I want to know what it's like to be the whole me,

not the 'me' in parts and pieces. But I also want to

know more about those deeper currents of flowing

magma that push along the tectonic plates of the

soul, forming and reforming mountain ranges and

ocean trenches, piling continent upon landmass,

slowly creating and re-creating the foundation

and structure and superstructure of a single

insignificant conscious entity: me."

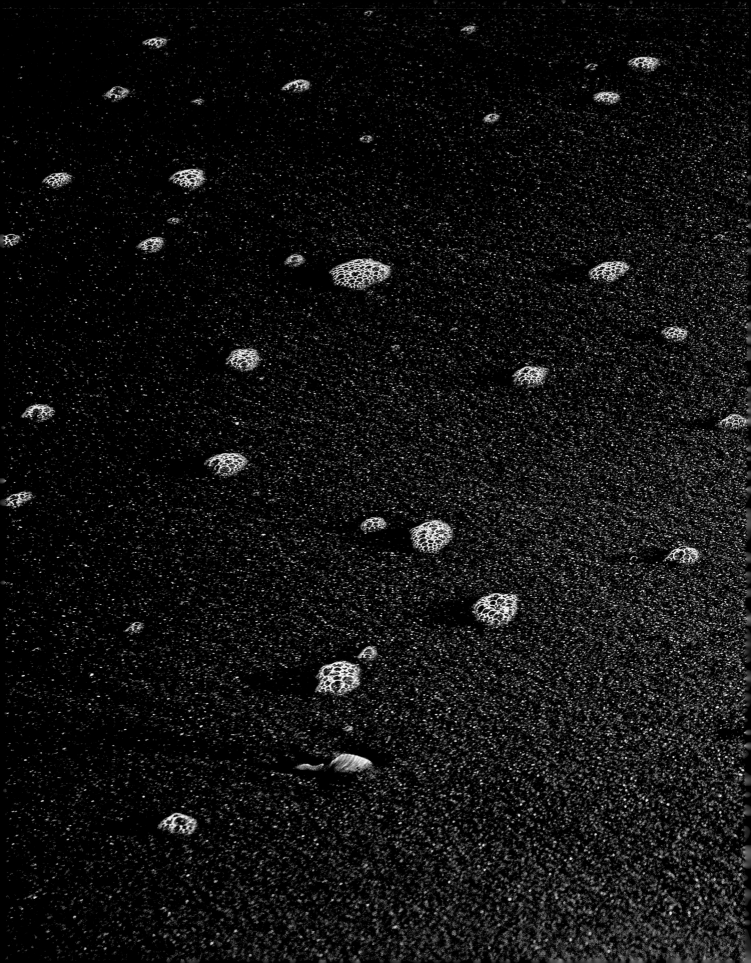

I GIVE MY EYES...

stories + conversations + dreams

Brian H. Peterson

Due Santi

Published by Due Santi Press
Bethlehem, Pennsylvania
www.DueSanti.org

ISBN 978-0-9990375-1-5

Design: Sherilyn Kulesh, Kulesh Design Group
Editing: Paula Brisco
Printing: Brilliant Graphics

Unless otherwise indicated, the images in
this book are photographs by the author.
Additional image captions are found on page 171.

Mr. Peterson is represented by
Santa Bannon/Fine Art,
Bethlehem, Pennsylvania.
www.santafineart.com

CONTENTS

To John and Jan
AD PUGNAM

Prologue: God Talks?

I used to talk to the sun as if it were God, called it Father, felt its presence inside as much as outside. I asked it questions. Once in a while, I heard answers.

You might as well know this about me now, in case you think only someone certifiably insane would admit to such things. A book is not just information, it's a meeting of minds, a friendship, and friends have to be real with each other, right? Do you want to tackle a book by someone who knows his grip on reality is that flimsy—and who apparently doesn't care?

By the way, I don't just write books—there's a freakin' library named after me. I am proud of the honor. But the thought of my name in vinyl letters on a museum wall makes my face grow moderately pink if not full-bore embarrassed red. As if attaching my name to something will make me any less dead when it's my turn to be dead!

Naked narcissism isn't my only source of discomfort. I love books and have bled several gallons of my life's blood making books. If I hadn't written this one—and let's say you gave it to me as a birthday present—I would want to read it and would fully intend to read it, but nowadays I rarely find "read a book" at the top of my to-do list.

People often give me books, assuming that, because I like to make them, I'd be curious about how other people get the job done. I've learned to dash off an e-mail quickly, so I can say thanks without including such courteous details as "snappy prose style" or "always wanted to know more about what Picasso had for breakfast." The sooner the response, the better the chances that I can express my gratitude without needing to remember what Pablo was doing with whom in 1907 while dreaming up cubism.

If someone gave you *this* book, my advice—considering the subject, size, etc.—is to get the thank-you out in a week. Two weeks, risky, and three—you'd better mention a detail or two from the book so you'll have some credibility when you say, "Really enjoyed it so far."

Because I'm such a nice guy, I'll throw a few snippets your way, suitable for a thank-you note. "The story about his dog Rufus is a real tearjerker." Or, to aim high, how about: "The magic of the sunrise over a North Carolina beach is revealed in ecstatic prose worthy of Ralph Waldo Emerson." The authoritative tone isn't right for you? "Not so sure about all those phone calls with God, but this guy asks the tough questions and doesn't pull any punches."

But be careful. You don't know me well yet—can you trust that I'm giving you actual information about my book? What if I'm really a bitter old misanthrope taking pleasure in messing with people who only pretend to read my brilliant wordsmithing? Or consider this:

maybe the person who gave *you* the book is just like me—i.e., loves to read but rarely gets around to the actual doing—and this person felt badly because, you know, the book looked interesting and has those pretty pictures of the ocean, and giving a meaningful book to a friend is almost as good as reading it, maybe even better when you think about it . . .

Guilt. It's literature's dirty little secret. I wonder what percentage of a publisher's revenue is generated by people whose guilty feelings about *not* reading a book make them gift it to their friends. As a pretend reader myself (who's just come out of the closet), I'm an expert on this psychological disorder—call it "dysfunctional literopathy"—but as a writer, I must confess that I'm the archetype, the Mount Everest of vectors propagating this pervasive syndrome.

I love to give my books away to anyone who grins in my direction or sells me a half-decent pair of shoes. I feel guilty burdening these good people with my pride and joy, but I can't help myself. So I take them off the hook by saying something cute like, "Your book report's due in a week." Because I'm so low-key about it, I probably make them feel even *more* guilty as they stare at the book for a while, until finally the thought occurs, "You know, I bet my friends would like it . . ."

If this strikes you as an overly pessimistic description of the joys and sorrows of the written word, then understand that the "literary guilt" riff is just a tongue-in-cheek way of introducing my mission, my Holy Grail if you will. I want to write a serious book that people might look forward to picking up once in a while—a book that can be read in one big swoosh or in dribs and drabs over months and years, a book where readers know they've entered a guilt-free zone. I don't care where, when, or how people read my words. I only care that the words be honest, the connection real, and that we all part company a little better off for making the effort.

I want you to know that I'm not proud of it. Being a pretend reader. I used to do it all the time. Read, that is. I fell in love with books constantly, couldn't get enough, always had to have more, read the whole output of a few authors, dabbled in philosophy, history, and aesthetics, even took courses so I could read more books.

Sometimes now I surprise myself with the random ideas and facts packed into my neurons from books I've read—but my knowledge tree could use some fresh soil and fertilizer. That's a fancy way of saying I need to slow down and start reading again. Not today, though. Not today.

It's a poor excuse, but I stopped reading books when I started trying to change the world. I needed the energy. Every single BTU my cells could produce.

Plenty of people do what I did—try to change the world—but I was a serious artist with a full-time job, and I kept on doing the art thing day after day, for a long time. Decades. I was a disciplined maniac. I learned the precise way to structure my day so I'd have a fighting chance of getting some work done, what I considered my *real* work, and I learned how to conserve every scintilla of energy so I could keep making images and weaving words.

Change the world? I sense contrary vibes drifting up through my keyboard's crevices. "Dude," says the skeptical voice, "first you said you're some weird-ass wild man on the edge of sanity who had conversations with God, and suddenly you're so busy that you need a personal secretary just to keep your desk organized? Why not fess up and tell your friendly reader that you also built King Tut's pyramid and were Charlemagne's masseuse?"

I know how silly those three words sound—"change the world"—but they're the best way to describe how I felt, though I'd never have dared to say them at the time, not even to myself.

I saw things happening that I liked, and things I didn't like, and I tried to cook up more of the former and in the process hoped that people would decide to do less of the latter. By "the world," I mean my world, the world I lived in, the world of art and culture and history, in a particular place—Philadelphia—at a particular time in a particular community.

How successful was I in this modest little mission? Remains to be seen. Come back in a hundred years, a thousand, follow a hundred thousand threads woven through a million intersecting lifetimes and add it all up and the answer is—c'mon, you said you were going to be real with your reader. No individual life can change the earth's path through the Milky Way galaxy or make the planet rotate in any direction other than counterclockwise.

True—but each of us can grab an oar and try to help the boat we're on navigate the currents on that turning earth. There's no way to measure such things objectively. I've done my share of rowing, would be a reasonable assessment. Done my share, and have the calluses to prove it.

Someone I worked with once told me I have a "lust for projects." Okay, that's fair. Sometimes they almost seemed to spring up on their own, but more often than not I cooked them up out of the sheer joy of making things happen. Eventually I helped to build a museum, really threw myself into it, tried to turn my part of the process into a private lab experiment whose goal was to see if what I believe in works in the real world—meaning it feeds people, makes a difference in people's lives, and perhaps even quietly, without fanfare, soul by soul, slowly, imperceptibly changes the world. Or at least the little corner of the cosmos that I called home.

Through it all—the memos and meetings, grant proposals and capital campaigns, budgets and timelines and strategic plans and exhibit scripts, I was still the crazy guy who used to talk to the sun as if it were God and made ecstatic pictures about light and way down deep was just trying to keep on singing my song.

How did the one me become the other me, or was there any "turning into," or was it all the same life lived? I guess that's one reason why I need to write this book.

Other books I've done were meant more as gifts, the best I can offer to anyone within earshot. This one—I promised I was going to put my cards on the table, treat you as a friend—this one is for *me*. It's a way of following the threads of my life as far as I can, forward and back, and seeing how they tie together.

This book includes stories and vignettes, an informal essay or two, snippets of an exhibit script, a transcribed conversation, a eulogy, a farewell, an e-mail exchange, some loose collections of words optimistically described as poems, and a lot of personal history—but mostly history on the inside, not the outside. As a palate-cleanser for all the navel gazing I included a book review from my professional life, and to add a little spice I threw in a sermon.

If I thought it up, made it, and still like it, then I'm going to trust that it belongs here and that the whole thing will hang together. And maybe have a decent chance of stirring up a few sympathetic vibrations elsewhere.

I considered exploring this landscape via the fiction route, but it didn't feel right. Besides, I had a conversation with God about this book. Well, not really. I use the word "God" without any clear idea what it means. "God" is a mark on a printed page, signifying some sort of experience that hardly seems shared given all the wars fought over it. And how can a single word ever encompass *that* particular experience? It's like giving a bear hug to a mountain range, or asking a brontosaurus what it feels like to be a flea.

These so-called "conversations"—the ones I'm aware of—don't happen every day, and there are no brass bands involved, or heavenly choirs. It's more like maneuvering a dinghy on the ocean in a fog at night, trying to keep an eye on a distant lighthouse while struggling to stay afloat.

I have choices. I'm not sure which path to take. I wrestle with the situation I'm in, consider my options, wrestle some more, and listen. In the listening is a question that I don't even quite know I'm asking. Then a kind of "answer" appears, and at least I can get a sense of what the question is, but it's usually more like a door opening than a "do this" or "do that." Or I may have turned in a new direction where I can find an answer. If there is one.

Write myself. Write my life. Those were the words that scrolled up my interior movie screen.

So that's what I'm doing. Not because some mysterious voice told me to, but because I took a hard look at what's necessary. Now. For me. I'm glad the voice is in there, quietly helping things along, occasionally providing a hint unasked for or giving me a tap on the shoulder if I start to wander. But I'm not a passive recipient of wise sayings from on high.

This is me, Brian, writing this book. I make decisions, stand by them, or change my mind when it's called for.

True. But that's not the whole picture.

This is hard to explain. Everything I do that matters is not done by me alone but by me together. Don't ask me who or what that "together" happens to be. None of the usual words come close to describing what it's like. That's another reason I need to write this book.

I want to know what it's like to be the *whole* me, not the "me" in parts and pieces. But I also want to know more about those deeper currents of flowing magma that push along the tectonic plates of the soul, forming and reforming mountain ranges and ocean trenches, piling continent upon landmass, slowly creating and re-creating the foundation and structure and superstructure of a single insignificant conscious entity: me.

Where does the me stop and the not-me start up, or are stop and start, here and there, just ink on a page, spots on a monitor? How do I know which words are the ones that open doors and windows and let something real drift over from me to you, and maybe back again?

The heavens are silent. Better just to listen. For what, from whom?

Don't know.

Listen. And live. The words will come.

Hello, Good-bye

How old am I? Let's say sixty. I'll retire at sixty-four. Inflation: how about three percent. Rate of return: five percent should be enough. Desired income? Go for the gusto—a hundred K.

Include Social Security—check.

Include outside income—check.

Include current retirement savings—check.

Estimated years of retirement—who thought up *that* category? Somebody who steps in cow manure and calls it apple pie.

Calculate. The screen says CALCULATE. Go ahead, Rambo—pull the trigger. Click that mighty mouse. Hmm—look at the clever graph. Wait a minute, those lines, those pretty little lines—they're heading in the wrong direction.

"YOUR ESTIMATED RETIREMENT INCOME IS NOT ENOUGH TO MEET YOUR NEEDS PROJECTION." The whole sentence is bright red with big letters. Not good.

I can almost hear Ray Charles, with that world-weary, wistful voice, crooning out his own version: "There's what you need, and there's what you got. And brother, you sure don't got nothin' yet."

Whatever. I can make the numbers dance. I can make those pie charts sing. Rate of return: six percent, not five. Years of retirement—let's settle for twenty instead of twenty-five . . .

The sky gradually brightens, the birds chatter and chirp, cars whiz by my window, a dog barks at a jogger. I've now reached the third page of Google hits on "retirement calculators." Fourth page, fifth page. Ten or twelve hits per page, each one a reminder that what happens tomorrow is a book being written. The final chapter is always the same.

But I am mighty. I am relentless.

I will defeat the armies of contingency. Click-click. I will conquer worst-case scenarios. Clackety-clack.

I am God's Holy Warrior of Mother-Clicking Doom. I thrust and parry, hack and slash until my enemies' bloody corpses are scattered before me. The future—you are *mine*. I *own* you. Obey me. Kneel before Brian.

I am the Prince of Denmark himself: a twenty-first-century Hamlet armed with a wireless mouse instead of a poison-tipped sword. Enough already with the griping about outrageous fortune. To be or not to be—get over it! That stuff is for losers. Hamlet—friend—you gotta get your gloomy ass out of that drafty Danish castle and into one of those perfect communities where everybody's smiling and dandelions are extinct—and where people who hit sixty-five just find the right retirement calculator, do the math, and live happily ever after.

It's not as though I wasn't warned. My brother did his best to describe her condition to me over the phone. He said she could no longer walk or talk, could barely get out of bed, and wasn't eating much. She was so far gone that hospice had taken her on with no questions asked.

I'd seen her at Christmas, and at least she recognized me. She still managed to have a conversation, as long as you didn't mind answering the same question about twenty-five times. To entertain myself, I started to make stuff up.

"Is this letter from you?" No, Ma, the Pope sent it, he says he wants to move to Arizona.

"Is this your letter?" Nope, that's from Albert Einstein, he says $E = mc^2$ was a big mistake.

"Whose letter is this?" It's from President Roosevelt. He says we have plenty to fear besides fear itself, so go ahead, be afraid. Be *very* afraid.

There was enough left of her personality to make her cranky, and she still refused to let people help her in the morning. "Help" meant getting her dirty diaper off and keeping an eye on her while she took a shower. She hated that diaper. But when the nurses discovered that she was hiding newspapers and toilet paper under her sheets to soak up the nightly discharge, they got the diaper on whether she liked it or not.

Finally her failing sense of balance went from failing to officially kaput, and she fell. They found her in the bathroom, bruised and unconscious, and sent her to the hospital, where what was left of her barely functioning brain turned to oatmeal.

I already had plane tickets to Arizona for her birthday in early June, and it was an open question if she would last that long.

She did. More or less.

One good thing about advanced dementia—birthday presents are no longer a problem. My brother and I stopped in the grocery store and picked up some flowers and festive balloons, then headed to the funny farm, aka Serenity—the river of no return, where the poor souls go whose failed neurons make them dangerous to themselves and others. I've made a hobby out of collecting the names of these places. Serenity is in my top three, along with "Golden Living." My favorite is the psych ward for seniors where my mother lived for a couple weeks while recovering from a seizure. When I called the switchboard, the cheerful voice announced, "Senior Lifestyles, where may I direct your call?"

As soon as we marched into Mom's room, I could see it was a mistake. She had no idea what a birthday was or who we were. Two strange men invading her world, singing a strange song, bearing strange objects—this was more than she could handle. She looked away, her face went blank, and she started to rub her bottom lip with thumb and forefinger.

When the song was mercifully over, we sat across from her and tried to draw her out. "Hey—how's the birthday girl?" Silence. "How are you feeling today?" Silence. "Your sister called last night." Silence, a blank stare, and more lip rubbing.

How did this happen? Where did this person come from? Whatever you could say about Gladys M. Peterson, she knew how to command a room. When your attention wandered while she was talking, she let you know. If you didn't say "uh-huh" every ten or fifteen seconds during a phone call, she would ask, "Are you there?"

The first time my wife Helen had the full Gladys experience, she told me it felt like a struggling butterfly must feel, pinned to a mounting board in an entomologist's laboratory. From then on, the word "pinned" entered our marital lexicon, used whenever we needed to describe the feeling of being trapped and inspected, with every flaw revealed.

Five years earlier Mom had the occasional memory lapse and got irate if we suggested that she might want to talk to a doctor about it. Three years earlier Mom didn't know where she was half the time and needed her husband to fill in the gaps, but at least she could still pretend there was nothing wrong. Now Mom was the potato formerly known as Gladys. A potato with feelings. A potato who was still alive, but everything she needed to *be* alive had been taken away.

I'm not the kind of person who gets angry with God at the injustices of the world. But if I were looking for an easy way to jackhammer the concept of a benevolent deity, then what Alzheimer's does to an ornery, complicated person like my mother would pretty much be "case closed." There is no discernible reason why this kind of suffering should be inflicted on a human being. None.

I saw her only a few times that birthday week, and each time the visit got shorter. I finally realized that she now had a new family—the people she saw every morning and every evening, who fed her, washed her, and comforted her.

For Gladys, whose memories were a dry creek in an endless desert, familiar had *become* family.

The day before I flew home, I made the trip to Serenity one more time. It felt like I was voluntarily feeding my arm into a meat grinder. But against all logic, I got in my parents' old Ford and made the five-minute drive to hell.

That sounds melodramatic, but Serenity was an inferno of lost souls. They were lounging on chairs in the hallways, and I could see them in their rooms as I walked by—staring into space with slack jaws and dull eyes. The *loungers* were bad enough, but there were also the *drifters*, who did nothing but walk, incessantly muttering to themselves, turning in one direction or another at the whim of a misfiring synapse.

One day a lady drifter wandered through Mom's open door. My brother, who was used to these interruptions, tried to nudge our guest toward the hallway, but she stood her ground. Finally a nurse walked by and called out her name, sharply, as if she were a dog begging for scraps under the dinner table. Obediently she turned and marched out.

When I walked through the padlocked door of Serenity for the last time, the chair in my mother's room was empty. Sometimes the caregivers wheeled their Idaho spuds into the kitchen to give them a change of scene. Sure enough, there was Gladys, slumped in a wheelchair, gazing up at a *Jeopardy!* rerun. I stood beside her for a few seconds, taking in her crumpled body, her mottled and folded skin just visible above the top of her robe, and her short, thin hair that Serenity's hairdresser had dyed a ghastly brown.

How do you say hello for the last time to someone you love so deeply that the love is like an invisible concrete foundation that keeps your house from crumbling to dust? How do you say hello to someone who is there but already gone, who felt your first kicks inside her, who taught you to read, who changed your diapers and fed you breakfast and despite her own wounds and troubles loved you as only a mother can love her child? How do you say hello?

How do you say good-bye to someone you never knew because she'd kept the door to her own private Serenity locked so tight that even she had forgotten the innocent little girl who lived there, who *still* lived there, despite crumpled body and lifeless eyes? How do you say good-bye to someone who never understood the damage she did because she didn't understand herself? Someone you love and always will love as only a child can love a mother? How do you say good-bye?

"Hi Mom."

She turned her head away from the TV and looked up at me. Suddenly, for the briefest of moments, her blank features formed into a look of—not recognition—but gladness, warmth. Someone had turned on a night light in a dark and empty house. A final puff of wind ruffled the leaves of a tree after a storm had passed. Only a flash, a zephyr, and then it was gone.

I wheeled her to her room and tried to have a conversation, but I knew the kindest thing I could do was leave. So I took her back to the kitchen and pointed her toward the TV.

"Bye Mom."

The nice man who opened Serenity's locked door glanced at me while he punched in the combination.

"How's your day going?"

"Well, it was fine until a few minutes ago."

The look on my face told him all he needed to know. He touched my arm gently and said, "It's a lot harder for us than it is for them."

My brother and I joke with each other now about who will be the last man standing, or maybe, *drifting*. The odds are not very good. All four siblings in my mother's family had dementia; Mom's father had it; her cousin had it. I've trained my neurologist to be honest, and when I told her about what I'd experienced in Arizona, she said, rather casually, "You know, just because you have Parkinson's doesn't mean you can't get Alzheimer's too."

So I stare at my computer in the wee hours, clicking and double-clicking. The logical part of my brain says I need to make well-informed financial decisions. But actually I do it because I want my mommy. And my daddy. I want those two people to still be in the world, somewhere, loving me the way they did, because it makes me feel safe.

A few days after I got home, on a Friday night around midnight, my brother called and said Mom had gone into some sort of respiratory distress. They were about to give her a shot of morphine to ease the discomfort but she stopped breathing and that was that.

He was in California visiting a sick friend, and I was a couple thousand miles away in Pennsylvania. I was haunted by the idea that our mother was alone when she died. She was such a sweet, fragile soul toward the end. To die by herself, with no family around—that was a terrible thing. But eventually I spoke with the nurse who was on duty that night. She filled in some of the details and said, "I want you to know that Gladys wasn't alone, and I held her hand until she was gone."

A couple weeks later I got a card from a friend whose father had died of Alzheimer's. She said that toward the end she'd asked him, point-blank, "Do you know who I am?"

"No," he replied. "But I know I care about you very much."

Now, looking back, I can see that this was what my mother was feeling the last time I saw her. She could no longer put the words together to say it. But she felt it. And I carry that moment with me, like a peanut butter sandwich in my favorite lunch box.

Once in a while I open up the lunch box and take a bite of that precious sandwich, and I remember my mother, all that she was and wasn't, all I learned from her and all I had to unlearn. I remember her love, and my love, her failures and mine.

Remember, and forgive.

Being Heard

Catching butterflies. If I wanted to write a poem about poetry readings, I'd try to work that metaphor in somewhere.

Since my wife became a serious writer, I've heard poetry read in bars, galleries, restaurants, libraries, bookstores, even a corner deli. Poets are the bravest artists around. They spend untold lonely hours boiling language down to its essence. Then these solitary wordsmiths are expected to go onstage and read their alchemically distilled verbiage as if they were Olivier or Gielgud playing King Lear.

After an hour or two of absorbing all those fast-moving words that leap and pirouette, dip and dive, almost within reach but just beyond my grasp—that's when I imagine myself in a meadow chasing an endless stream of butterflies. So many beautiful words, bobbing and bouncing in the air, but no net to catch them, and then—where did they go?

Once in a while, the butterflies turn into arrows aimed at me by a skilled archer. When they find their target, they stick.

The reading by the woman who nearly died of cancer—that one, I remember. The way she owned her suffering, didn't run from it, but didn't sit comfortably in its house wearing robe and slippers. The way she stood up, tall and strong, held nothing back, but did it all so gracefully, with nuance and timing, an unfolding story, each poem another chapter. I wept. Couldn't help myself, the words were so necessary, so true.

Afterward I thanked her and tried to describe how her performance had affected me, but she was worried that she'd been self-indulgent, revealed too much. We talked briefly about people's reactions to illness, how friends begin to make decisions for us, slowly stripping away our independence and dignity. I said, "When this happens, I become a fan of Dylan Thomas." She nodded and excused herself when another poet walked by.

Rage, rage against the dying of the light. Brave words. But later, as I was closing down my laptop and settling in for the night, I began to wonder. I take five drugs to reduce Parkinson's symptoms. One of them regularly causes people to do strange things they can't control. Obsessive stuff like shopping, gambling, sex, even piling and unpiling household objects, hours at a time. When patients stop taking the drug, the weirdness stops too.

My dosage is double what most people can tolerate, and I've been downing these pills every day for the better part of a decade. They've probably kept me functional. But no one knows what drug-induced mischief might be going on between my ears.

As I drift off to sleep, I wonder: Will I know the difference between dream and reality tonight? And if I work up a healthy snit about the dying of the light, who's doing the raging? The drugs, the illness, or me? How do I know? How do others know who read my words? How could I dare to speak in the public arena, show my work, write books, and expect others to take me seriously . . .

Suddenly I'm awake . . . but where am I? Eyes slowly open. Something's moving, sliding. Sliding faster . . . falling . . . Suddenly a hand flies out. *Bang!* Fingers close on metal. Got it. That's *my* hand—grabbed something in midair. Fully present now, I slowly lay my laptop down, gently, gently, then let go.

Eyeballing the distance and imagining the impact, I ask, what just happened? Woke up from a deep sleep just as my expensive computer with my whole life inside was beginning its rapid descent toward oblivion. My body knew what to do and did it. Quicker than thought. Like a frog's tongue flicking out and snatching a juicy fly in midair.

The feeling suddenly rose up, an electric surge of unstoppable conviction.

I don't know about tomorrow. But today, I'm here. *I will stand up and say what I need to say.*

Echo

I spotted them in the ticket line. They were roughly the same age—early fifties. She was stocky, with graying hair. Red patches on her forehead and chin. She had the lined face of a weary soldier on the front lines who woke up every morning and asked, "What's going wrong today?"

Much had gone wrong already. That was clear. Her husband was wearing a bright orange T-shirt, short pants, sneakers, and a baseball cap. Might have been headed for a golf vacation in the Bahamas, but this guy hadn't played golf in a long time. He sat stiffly, stared straight ahead, eyes blank, face expressionless except for a vague feeling of panic that reminded me of my dog at the vet's office.

I wondered—of all the things that can put somebody in an airport wheelchair—could it be—no, too much of a coincidence. But sure enough, his chin—there it was, a telltale tremor. He was trying to control it, but his mouth was slowly vibrating, up and down, like the Adam's apple of a soprano when she hits a high note.

Definitely not the Bahamas. They were traveling for the same reason I was: a family member was graduating from college. I overheard the lady's conversation with a person standing nearby—one of those random exchanges that spring up when people who don't know each other have time to kill.

Seconds, dragging into minutes, inching into an hour or two. The panic on wheelchair man's face—no longer vague. The memory of the first time I'd felt a hint of that panic came back to me in a rush.

I was standing in a grocery store on the first day of the first serious drug, a half hour after taking the first miniscule dose, which the drug company had provided free of charge along with gradually increasing weekly dosages in small plastic bottles.

"How can they afford to give all this stuff away?" I had asked my doctor. She smiled and said, "They know what they're doing."

I was in the produce section when the drug kicked in. For a minute or two, the carrots and cucumbers wavered, the floor seemed oddly tilted, and the shopping cart became my life preserver. I got a few funny looks when the storm passed. Not that I blamed people for wondering why someone would suddenly freak out near the fresh vegetables.

A clever person might have said, "Watch out for the rutabagas—they're sure packin' a wallop today!" But who could come up with a zinger right after their first drug-induced dopaminergic funk? A snappy one-liner wouldn't have made that moment any easier. This thing was real.

There's only one good thing about a delayed flight—it's easier to make friends. Odd how shared suffering does that—opens people up—even when the problem is nothing more than the boredom of standing around for a few hours in an airport.

The airline lady finally announced that the plane had arrived and we'd be boarding in ten minutes. Thirty minutes went by. Phone calls and frustration behind the counter. Eventually airline lady opened the door to the Jetway and disappeared. Door opened. She grabbed the microphone and announced that the crew was not on the plane. A dozen conversations started up within earshot: "Gee, I guess the planes fly themselves now" and "I think I saw them in the bar" and "Must be in the bathroom with the flight attendant."

I glanced over at wheelchair man. The tremors had evolved into random vibrations of shoulders and arms, with occasional jerks and twists of head and torso. Poor guy, airports are tough, I thought. My first plane ride after I got the bad news . . . I think I had gone through five or six of those weekly pill bottles, without a repeat of the grocery store loveliness.

Delayed takeoff, missed connection, long lines, then the airport hotel. The usual story. I knew I wasn't the clearest bell in the bell choir the next day as I was boarding a sunrise flight.

But I wasn't expecting what happened as the plane was taxiing to the runway: the kind of big-time, bona fide drug reaction that I'd read about in the fine print section of the manufacturer's specs (yes, I read the whole thing). I was certain that any second my breakfast would be sprayed throughout the cabin. And there was nothing I could do but desperately rummage through the seat pocket looking for the barf bag while the guy to my right looked on with poorly concealed dread.

Both of us (barf bag and I) lived to fight another day. But in the snapshot my parents took when I landed, I was a pale, sickly green. That was the day when officially, in my own eyes, I became a sick person.

All the minor aggravations of getting from one place to another—the delays, the security, the airport crowds—are annoying for folks whose brains work normally but terrifying for anybody who isn't sure from one minute to the next what fresh torment their bodies are going to devise.

That fear was the source of the panic I saw in wheelchair man's eyes. But he also had a childlike sweetness that didn't fit with his love handles and five o'clock shadow. It was the look of a man who'd grown used to people taking care of him because he'd forgotten how to take care of himself.

Finally the plane was ready, and we started the boarding ritual. Wheelchair guy went first. He passed the test when they asked if anybody needed assistance. I was not too far behind him, so I could see the commotion as they prepared to carry him on board. Then another ten minutes went by. Finally the airline lady emerged from the plane, looking like she'd just run a marathon, and we all trudged inside. My seat was toward the back.

I glanced down when I walked by him, and I could see the thick beads of sweat on his face. His arms were shaking violently, and his shoulders were hunched forward, as if they were carrying a hundred-pound sack of flour.

My brother was waiting for me at the luggage carousel. Wheelchair guy and his wife were there too, looking relieved, exhausted, angry. It would have been a lot easier for these people to stay home. But they had made the trip. Interesting.

Now I wish I'd spoken to him, learned his name, heard his story. Chances are he was still in there, enough to make eye contact, say hello. I could have learned a few things from him, maybe helped him feel less alone. But I was afraid and kept my distance.

They had found their luggage and made their way to the door by the time my suitcase finally popped through the rubber curtain. I hadn't planned on saying anything, but the words came out.

"Did you see the guy in the wheelchair? Looked like he was going to Hawaii?"

"Yeah, he was in pretty bad shape. What was his problem?"

"Major league Parkinson's. Major league." Instinctively my brother reached down for my suitcase. I waved him off, but he insisted.

"It's okay—I'm fine." He knew I was lying, and I knew that he knew I was lying. But that moment, that day, the lie was looking pretty good. A lot better than the truth. We glanced at each other, smiled. He let go of my bag and said, "What's in there, an anvil?" "Hey old-timer, the darned things have wheels nowadays," I replied as I grabbed the bag, extended the handle, and followed him out the door.

A Wise Soul Who Died Well

Dog stories have a few basic ingredients: This is how Dog entered our lives. These are Dog's adorable idiosyncrasies. Then we had this problem or that problem, making us love Dog all the more. Dog goes away, has great adventures and miraculously returns, and/or Dog dies, preferably after long illness, but not before saving a baby from a grizzly bear. Only then do we see what Dog taught us, and isn't it wonderful that *we* learned it from a dog?

We don't need no Sock-ra-teeze to teach *us* about the meaning of life. And we don't need no high-and-mighty pooch like Lassie or Rin Tin Tin neither. No siree, any ol' mutt will do.

I don't mind the heroics or the over-the-top affection. I know what it feels like to love a dog. It's that cloying molasses at the end that bothers me. Dog stories pretend to be about dogs, but are really about us. There's rarely any honest curiosity about what it's like to *be* a dog.

A dog is, basically, a slave. We buy and sell them. We breed them. To live in our world, dogs learn to give us what we need. They reside in our homes but only if they remember our rules. Those who fail rarely survive. You can be cruel to a dog—not too cruel, though, and cute little puppies are off-limits, or you might end up with your mug shot in the paper.

Yes, we grant them a certain degree of personhood. Dogs have feelings—but they're not human, right? Those people who wonder if they'll be reunited with Fido in heaven—they're plumb loco, right?

I have no answers. All I can do is tell my dog story.

Rufus was not a ball of fluff who survived by looking cute, or a canine version of Hulk Hogan. Rufus had legs, and he loved to run. If he'd been cooped up for a while, sometimes he shot out the back door, jumped the steps onto the lawn, and flew around the yard in big wide circles, hair and tail sailing in the wind, tiny tufts of grass popping up as those four graceful limbs pumped the ground.

We learned to always, always check for deer before letting him out, because the deer drove Rufus mad. He'd hoist himself up by his front paws so he could scan the backyard through the kitchen window, and if he spotted deer in the distance, the yelping and yowling began, followed by groaning and growling, capped off by moping and glaring.

Occasionally we took pity on him and opened the door. He blasted across the lawn, startled deer arrayed before him, and we watched with terror and wonder as this blur of pure animal mobility streaked toward the invisible prison wall. Suddenly he turned his body around midstride, dug in his paws, and somehow avoided being tweaked by the gadget strapped to his neck.

Rufus broke out of jail three times. Twice by bolting for an open door at a kennel, and once when he stepped on a window switch in Helen's car, lowered the window, and jumped out of a moving vehicle into rush-hour traffic. Helen tried desperately to keep an eye on him, but her Volvo was a rhino chasing a gazelle.

We thought we'd lost him. Finally he ran out of gas, stopped running, and a nice person spotted the phone number on his tag and called us.

After that near disaster, our vet installed one of those subcutaneous GPS devices. And we made sure our backseat window switches were deactivated. Rufus never escaped again, but he still perched himself by the window and plastered his nose against the glass, making strange-looking splotches that glowed in the sunlight.

We never learned how old he was or deciphered his particular mixture of genes and chromosomes (two parts border collie with a smidge of Brittany spaniel?). Wherever he entered the world, he didn't stay there long. This dog was born to run.

Rufus was found by the side of a Kansas City highway with a broken leg. The guy who saved his life already had several dogs and didn't need more, so he put Rufus up for adoption on one of those doggy websites.

We got Rufus because we felt guilty leaving our other dog in the kitchen all day by himself. That brilliant idea didn't work out too well. Our canine friends were like warriors in a Greek tragedy, doomed by cruel gods to hack away at each other until the end of time.

Actually they rarely fought. But when we let them out, they'd peel off in opposite directions and pretend the other one didn't exist. They disliked each other from the first day to the last, and there was nothing we could do about it.

They declared a truce only when they spotted a groundhog who'd wandered too far from the safety of his den. Then our adorable bundles of unconditional love turned into a canine attack machine—one performing a perfect decoy move while the other darted in from behind, snarling and snapping. When the desperate varmint turned to protect his exposed flank the first dog went straight for the jugular. It was over in a few seconds.

The victorious gladiators had no idea what to do with the murdered Punxsutawney Phil, but when I heard the commotion I always ran into the yard and claimed the body. They expected this from the alpha male. I figured that if they got a taste of groundhog, they might begin to think about a more flavorful cuisine than canned dog food. Seeing this elegant dance of mayhem and death embedded in the genes of two suburban pets, I decided to avoid activities that took me anywhere near a wolf pack or hungry hyenas.

Who are these animals that sit on our laps and daintily dance with their trainers at the Westminster dog show? Do we really want to know?

We picked up Rufus near a turnpike exit a couple hours east of our house. He'd been transferred from crate after crate into car after car by a bunch of dedicated people who didn't know each other but were part of a transport system set up by the doggy website. For a creature who dreamed of freedom, this was the most effective form of torture—cooped up in a succession of cages, manhandled by strangers, and subjected to a barrage of nasty smells like fresh asphalt and diesel exhaust.

The dog was a mess. We had to feed him a special blend of white rice and hamburger to stop the diarrhea, and at first his fur was unpleasant to touch, scratchy and coarse.

But when he finally got better, the hair behind his ears became soft and thick, and I could feel the muscles beneath his skin when I gave him a little rubdown. What a magnificent creature he was, fur trailing behind him, head held high. We began to call him King Rufus, because he looked the part and acted it. Feeding this pet was like trying to get a wine connoisseur to drink day-old rotgut from a brown paper bag. Instead of wolfing down his dinner like a normal dog, he made a point of sticking his nose into the bowl, then walking into the next room and pretending to sleep.

"Rufus, get in here and eat your dinner." No Rufus.

"RUFUS!"

Still no Rufus. When I poked my head around the corner to see where the heck he was, he'd raise his head and stare at me regally, then yawn.

"So that's the game you're playing, buster," I muttered to myself while I picked up his perfectly excellent dog vittles and put the wrapped-up bowl in the fridge. "Tomorrow's another day."

Then there were his crazy pills. The vet recommended two a day, and Rufus knew immediately how badly we wanted to get them down his throat. We tried cheese, peanut butter, and "guaranteed to work" tidbits from the pet store. In desperation we even hid the pill in a piece of salmon. He *loved* salmon. Finally, we thought, a surefire pill vector. It worked for a few days, then came that familiar haughty sniff. In desperation, Helen wrestled open his jaws and jammed the pill down his gullet. It was the only way.

Crazy pill? The first sign of trouble was in the car, a few weeks after we got him. We'd stopped at a red light, about to turn onto a busy street. Suddenly the dog was in the front seat, panting, legs frozen in place, eyes wide, his lips curled up in a look of pure panic. This behavior seemed less mysterious when, later, we remembered that he'd been found on a highway with a broken leg.

"I think this dog has PTSD," I said to Helen, while Rufus looked up at me and nuzzled my kneecap.

I should have figured out that a creature capable of a posttraumatic stress disorder panic attack might possess a depth of feeling not that different from ours.

It was easy to forget, however—that depth of feeling. The first few years were fine—we settled into a routine, and the highway-induced crisis never happened again. But then came the barking. He started up in the middle of the night, and nothing would make him stop. No amount of attention, no amount of treats, nothing—except what he really wanted, which was to go outside and run, or lie down in his favorite spot behind a bush on the side of the house.

We didn't know that was what he wanted, not at first. When we did figure it out, we still couldn't let him do it. There are laws where we live about dogs barking outside. Thirty minutes, and the neighbors can call the cops. So we had to keep him inside when we were gone.

One day I came home from work, ambled into my office to check my e-mails, and discovered that Rufus had not only attacked my closet, strewing its contents all over the floor, but with some bizarre, demented logic, had gone for the "memory box" that I kept on the floor. Letters from my long-dead grandmother, pictures of old friends, had been torn up and scattered around the room.

The next day we closed the door to my office, and he did the same thing to Helen's closet.

We tried barricading him in the kitchen with childproof gates. He bashed his head against them until the tough plastic mesh got dented and the wooden supports cracked.

Then somebody told us that that for dogs, a crate is like a den and makes them feel secure. So we tried a crate. He attacked the door, drawing blood from his lips and gums, and somehow managed to bend the steel rod that held the door shut. Neither of us could bend it back.

The worst moment was the day we attached him to a leash anchored under a leg of the kitchen table, reasoning that it might give him a bit more mobility than a crate. Helen called when I was driving home from work. "You need to see this," she said.

Not only had Rufus dragged the large wooden table across the floor, he'd managed to scatter great piles of magazines and other kitchen detritus everywhere. Then, in a final coup de grâce, he had peed and pooped in several places and mixed it all up into a smelly, disgusting stew.

We talked to a "dog whisperer," who diagnosed it as extreme separation anxiety. The vet agreed, so that's when we started the crazy pills. We were never sure they worked, because the troubles would die down for a while, then start up again, with no logic that we could see. But on any given day when we had to leave him inside, we didn't know what we'd find when we returned.

Finally, we gave up. If the weather was good, we left him outside. The neighbors were happy, and so was the dog.

Through it all, he never stopped nuzzling my knee, or coming out of his Rufus nest to greet me when I got home from work. And when I scratched his ear for a while, his head heated up like a toaster oven. "Must be an ear-ogenous zone," I said to Helen. "Yes," she replied. "He's having an ear-gasm."

There's a painting by George Bellows that shows an older couple sitting on a couch. The man stares vacantly into empty space. The woman leans slightly forward, both hands cradling a book, with a pained look on her face. Though only two or three feet apart, they're disconnected and alone.

I saw the painting once, in a book, and tried to describe it to Helen. "See, this is what happens to people like us if you're not careful," I told her. "You start out all lovey-dovey, but then you have to watch each other turn into old farts, and it's too damned scary."

Now that Rufus is gone, I can see that as he grew older, I had a harder and harder time giving him a scratch behind the ears when he nuzzled my knee. It didn't help that he destroyed my stuff, then peed on it. Let's just say that again in my defense. The dog was certifiable. Bonkers. I knew he wasn't born that way, that like me, his personality had been shaped by what he'd experienced. But were I not an educated citizen of the twenty-first century, I would be very comfortable with the concept that this mutt needed an exorcism.

Rufus was *my* dog. It's not that Helen didn't love him too, but he was a "guy's guy" kind of canine. He understood how men talk to each other. The other dog went straight for the ladies and always found a way to extract a tummy scratch or a treat. Rufus couldn't be bothered with such trivial things. He was "the King." He felt it, he knew it, and no one could ever convince him otherwise.

I identified with his kingliness. I liked it. And when he started to show his age, I turned away from him as surely as the dude in the Bellows painting turned away from his lonely wife.

How could the King become this doddering old geezer who slept most of the day and jumped up with a start when I walked up behind him and gave him a friendly pat on the butt?

He was stiff when he woke up, had a hard time with stairs, and his eyes were cloudy when he emerged from his nest to say hello. But then he'd get warmed up and race around the yard again, and for a few minutes nothing had changed.

His once-powerful back legs were now his biggest problem. Sometimes they stiffened, and even worse, occasionally they'd start to twitch involuntarily.

We were worried about those herky-jerky legs, so a few days before he died I took Rufus to the vet.

"Some sort of neurological issue, pretty common in older dogs."

The doc smiled when I replied, "Looks like the old boy's not ready for doggie heaven just yet." I knew my dog, I told myself. The only place he wanted to be was on our back porch, curled up in a beam of sunlight.

But he was also hiding something, putting on a show, and he was good at it. Never let 'em see the King sweat.

It's easy to fool somebody who wants to be fooled as badly as I did. Which was why, when the end finally came, it took me a while to figure out that he was in trouble.

I often work through the night, and usually the only sound is the quiet, steady breathing of sleeping animals. But that night, Rufus couldn't settle down. Eventually he maneuvered over to where I was sitting and stood there, frozen, panting. I couldn't take it in, how desperate he was—as if simply being near me would somehow make him feel better. Then I noticed that one of his front legs had stopped working. Instead of padding the ground, it dragged along like there were no bones inside.

Finally the other front leg gave out and he collapsed. He kept on trying to walk, but all he could do was stumble and slide and fall, then struggle up on his front elbows, then flop down on the floor like a rag doll.

He was the King. Still, he was the King. But now *he* was the desperate groundhog, with enemies all around and no way to escape. Finally I saw. I understood. Whatever was going on, this time there was no fixing it.

I went upstairs to wake up Helen, and holy hell, that dog was following me up the stairs.

"Oh Rufus, don't do that!" But the look on his face said, I'm coming. So I turned around and helped him. Dragged him, really, because he wasn't walking anymore.

It was four in the morning, but Helen must have heard the racket, because she was sitting up in bed, bleary-eyed, confused. "Babe, it's Rufus," I said. "He can't walk anymore."

We had a war council. I voted for taking him to the emergency vet hospital and getting it over with. Helen said no, let's see if he'll settle, and we'll call our vet in the morning. If it's his time to go, let him do it in a familiar place. Maybe, just maybe, he'd get better, and at least he'd have one more night at home, with us.

Somehow we got him downstairs, and finally he lay down and drifted off to sleep, with Helen dozing nearby on the couch.

We were lucky. It was "surgery day" at the vet's, which meant there would be no one in the waiting room, and they could see him later that morning. Fine—but how do we get him in the car when his legs didn't work?

"How about a blanket?" I asked.

But she'd already spread a beach towel on the floor. We shook him a little to wake him up. Helen rubbed his ears. "Okay, Rufie, how ya' doing?"

But nothing had changed. He tried to walk, and down he went.

Nothing had changed—but something *had* changed. This time, when he went down, he stayed down. The night before, he had fought like there was no tomorrow. Now, he knew. There *was* no tomorrow.

We maneuvered Rufus out the door, down the steps, and into the car. As we hoisted him onto the back seat, there was a loud thump and Helen stopped in midstride.

"Oh crap, did you bump your head?"

No need for a reply, as her shoulders sagged and she looked at me in exasperation, as if to say, Gee, ain't life just grand?

"We'll lay him on his back, on the floor," I said. "I'll stay here with him."

From our house to the vet's office—two minutes. I reached down and stuck my hand in his brown-and-white fur, until I found the soft place behind his ear and started scratching.

I looked at his face, his eyes, and then I stopped scratching and kept looking. I couldn't stop looking. I couldn't stop. This was my dog, my Rufus, whom I'd lived with every day for eleven years. But now—what was I seeing. *What was I seeing?*

He stared into empty space, eyes wide—a look of pure terror—at the same time, joy—no, not joy—it was concentration. He was awake. Just when he was about to leave, he was *here*. But no, no, he was here and also somewhere else.

Two minutes. I sat in the backseat of Helen's car and looked at him. He lay there, on the floor of the car, and looked at—what? *What was he seeing?*

What did he see through those cloudy eyes that now, at the end of his life, were clear, clear as the view from our kitchen window? But he wasn't looking at deer in the backyard anymore.

"Now we see through a glass, darkly, but then face to face." I can't believe I'm quoting Saint Paul in a lame attempt to describe how my dog looked when he was about to die. But that's the best explanation I can come up with.

Face to face, with—but I don't know, I can't know, until I get there myself.

It was terrifying to me, that look on Rufus's face, but also a gift. The gift of nakedness. There was no illusion left for this creature, just reality, which he was seeing, now, for the first time—and somehow, by being there, I was helping him see it.

Thankfully the vet didn't have back problems. He lifted Rufus gently off the floor, carried him inside, and laid him down on the examining table.

Quietly the doctor squeezed, prodded, stroked. But I knew he was doing it for us, not Rufus. He explained that older dogs sometimes rupture a spinal disc spontaneously, causing unbearable pain and loss of mobility.

"Look at the front legs," he said.

Not that we needed any convincing, but our dog's legs were like two baseball bats stuck to a sack of potatoes.

"We could give him some meds to relieve the pain, but—" and here the vet paused. "Treatment is not really an option, given his age and overall condition."

You could see in Rufus's eyes that he was ready to go. So we let him go.

We stroked him and wept over him and gave him our last little bit of love while the vet administered the shot in his leg. He breathed his final breath, licked his chops in a typical doggy way, and his legs finally relaxed, and then he was gone.

Driving home, I told Helen that I could see him, in my mind, chasing the deer as he loved to do in our backyard, but now there was no fence and he could run as far as he wanted, with no fear that he wouldn't find his way home again.

A couple weeks earlier I was sitting in our kitchen with some friends. Rufus wandered by on his way to the back door and his nest behind the bushes. But seeing us there, he stopped for a minute and stuck out his neck for an ear massage. Somebody said, "There it is, unconditional love."

Always on the lookout for the unpardonable cliché, I launched into a monologue about an article I read years ago in a science magazine on the subject of the neurological development of children, how they were unable to fully relate to the world unless their frontal lobes had matured, and until then, empathy and relationship were impossible.

"A dog is not capable of what we call love," I said, armed with all the confidence of the scientific mind. "They don't have the brainpower."

Now that confidence has gone away, replaced by the memory of the look on my dog's face during that two-minute journey to the Big Chill.

I no longer know what, or who, a dog is, or what, or who, we are. All I know is, a few minutes before saying good-bye, I saw my dog for who *he* really was, and he was a wise soul. Crazy as a loon, and nearly drove me crazy too. But he made up for it with the majesty and beauty of his death.

And that's the end of my dog story.

A wise soul he was, our Rufus. A wise soul who died well.

Conversation: Lost and Found

A conversation with John Weiss,
recorded at Weiss's home in Elkton, Maryland, January 11, 2011

When I met John Weiss in 1982, I was a year shy of thirty, and the only formal instruction I'd had in photography was a couple of noncredit evening classes at the University of Montana ten years earlier, plus an occasional critique or weekend workshop. He was in charge of the graduate photo program at the University of Delaware, and was a formidable figure in the photography world.

There was a minor issue with my plan to enter grad school in photography: that darned piece of paper called a bachelor's degree. Oh I had one, but mine was in music, not visual art. Most teachers would have pointed toward the door and said don't bother to apply. But a musician who wanted an MFA in photography was intriguing to John. I was a person with a story, who'd lived a little, probably had some imagination. More likely to have something to say than someone who'd taken the conventional path.

John Weiss, *Father and Daughter, Cuba,* 2014

42

His own path was anything but conventional, but the result was a gifted artist and master teacher who ran the grad program at Delaware for more than three decades. Over the years John and I discovered that while our personalities and habits were different, our experience of creativity—the daily discipline, the small successes and failures, the deep seriousness of the commitment—was intensely and surprisingly connected. I was often awestruck by John's simple ability to see: from corner to corner and side to side, absorbing every tiny detail of a visual event as it darts before his eye. Even more miraculous was his ability to turn perfect strangers into friends and partners, who together with him made images filled with love and generosity.

John and I often had memorable conversations about art and life that we promptly forgot, but one day on a whim we decided to grab an iPad and punch Record. Eventually we recorded

John Weiss, *Father and Son, Hadzabe People,* Tanzania, 2012

three. What follows is an excerpt of our first, also the best—more spontaneous, less self-conscious, and eventually landing on sacred ground: the artist's calling, how artists are "born," and how the creative life and the interior life, the life of the spirit, are so mysteriously woven together.

Peterson: Where were you before you discovered photography?

Weiss: My first love was playing ball. I loved team sports. I loved the idea of working together for the common welfare of one and all, carrying your own load, and working toward a common goal. Loved it.

Peterson: Baseball, right?

Weiss: Baseball, basketball, soccer, football, I played everything.

Peterson: You made it to the AA level or something—

43

Weiss: I'd like to say that, but it's not true.

Peterson: Was it "A" level? Babe Ruth?

Weiss: I made it to what's called semi-pro. This consists of failed minor leaguers who no longer are in the professional system, and wannabes like me who hope they can compete and get the chance to sign with a club.

Peterson: How much were you paid at the semi-pro level?

Weiss: Less than zero because I had to pay my own expenses to drive to Philadelphia.

Peterson: God, that's bad.

Weiss: I lasted one game. You get immediate feedback. I was pitching, and the batters tell you how good you are.

Peterson: I played Little League baseball, and when everybody hit puberty, that was the end of the line for me. The coach put me in as a pinch hitter, and there was this thirteen-year-old kid who probably weighed two hundred pounds. His name was Tiny Little Junior. Tiny threw a fastball right down the middle of the plate, and I jumped back. I was doomed.

Weiss: Well, here's what happened to me. I was a relief pitcher in the ninth inning. My team was up by three. I got two outs, a walk, the bases were loaded, then I got two strikes on the batter—and I threw him my Uncle Charlie, a 12–6 curve ball.

Peterson: It was the best you had.

Weiss: Dropped like a brick.

Peterson: And he saw it all the way.

Weiss: He saw it all the way, and it's still in orbit.

Peterson: *[laughter]* Somewhere in the Andromeda Galaxy maybe.

Weiss: I had my feedback, and I hung up my spikes.
　　　　Anyway, I was just filled with this passion to play ball. I just loved it, and then it was

over, and I was nothing from nowhere. I had no energy. I had no passion. It was gone.
Then I started working, and for lack of a better idea, making money.

Peterson: That was the bank, right?

Weiss: Insurance company in Hartford, Connecticut, and the bank in Boston.

Peterson: Does it still exist?

Weiss: Probably. If you could go back and find any of those employees who worked with me, they would universally say he was one weird dude, and we're happy that he's outta here.

Peterson: What was weird about you?

Weiss: Well, I didn't fit in. I wanted to fit in, but I didn't know how.

Peterson: Now, the dude I know is the last person who would ever want to fit in.

Weiss: I was let go by the insurance company after two months. I think I lasted thirteen months at the bank.

Peterson: John. Question. There's this romantic idea about an artist wrestling with the gods, going up on the mountain, suffering for humanity, all that crap. Is it crap? Is it ever possible for an artist to "fit in"?
Or is being an artist by definition a solitary journey? That's what I'm asking.

Weiss: Yep. That's my answer. Yep. Let me give you an example of an exquisitely good day for me. I get up in the morning and I go buy the paper at the local newsstand. There are several local newsstands. I go to one where there's no conversation. I've been going there ten years. They don't know my name. They don't even make eye contact.
Then I go home and print.

Peterson: John, there've been moments when I'm in the most intensive social situations, organizing things, doing things, and I suddenly realize that way down deep inside, I'm alone. There's a part of me that's totally untouched. Just strolling down its own little path. Listening.
But if it's all so solitary, then what about that story you told me, when you first fell in love with photography? It was something outside of you that really hit you and woke you up.

Weiss: We seek it out, don't we? We seek out that connection with things.

Peterson: What I'm thinking is, there has to be this core of self, of solitude, and it has nothing to do with how social you are or how engaged you are with your environment.

Weiss: I think you're right.

Peterson: There's a core of solitude, but you're also listening. Listening for that "still, small voice" inside, that can be hard to separate from the background static.

If there's too much static, how can you hear anything? When I'm really working, I'm always sort of "checking in" with myself, listening. Took me a long time to get those channels cleared out and get the juices flowing.

Weiss: That's part of the job description.

Peterson: Easier said than done … So what happened next? I know the outline—how about a little more detail.

Weiss: Well, one day I discovered photography. This is my little mantra: "I was born in Boston at the age of twenty-eight. My father was Minor White, and I named my mother Photography."

Peterson: *[pause]* Ooh.

Weiss: You can call it whatever you want, but that's my truth.

Peterson: Well, that's a bit over the top, but you know what, if you back it up with living the life, then more power to you.

I'm interrupting your story, but I remember the first day I came into your graduate class. You didn't come on like this nicey-nice guy who said, "Oh, we're all going to have this lovely time together, and then at the end, you'll all be artists, and it'll be great. You'll even have a master's degree."

You challenged us. You said something like, "Not only am I a photographer, I AM photography. I live photography. I honor photography. I worship at the altar of photography, and you people, you're not doing it." It sounded like arrogance, but I didn't mind.

I thought, "Well, this guy's got high standards, and he doesn't mind challenging me, and what he says is really coming from commitment and love." You were not going to lie to us and say it's easy.

Weiss:　　It came out of joy. It came out of pure belief in the truth of what I was saying and I guess was meant to set the bar.

Peterson:　That's exactly what I mean—and I didn't mind it a bit. I was in awe of it, to be quite honest. I really was.

Weiss:　　That's wonderful you shared that with me. That's your gift to me today. I had forgotten about that.

Peterson:　Okay, so let's go back to that day when you were "born." What happened on that day?

Weiss:　　Bri, before that day, I was a nonperson. I was desperately unemployed for almost a year. I couldn't get a job. Then I was offered a job in Boston at the bank.

Peterson:　So you went to Boston.

Weiss:　　To work at the bank. Boston, to me, really means Cambridge, and Cambridge still is an epicenter of energy and achievement and excitement. When I wasn't working, I'd hang out in Cambridge.

　　　　So Bri, it was a cold, cold wintry day.

Peterson:　What year, roughly?

Weiss.　　1968. So I'm driving on Massachusetts Avenue, and it's cold. Standing in this golden ray of sun I saw this beautiful, beautiful woman, the epitome of beauty.

　　　　She had her thumb up in the classic hitchhiking mode, and I thought to myself, "Who am I, if not a good Samaritan?"

Peterson:　She needed your assistance, clearly.

Weiss:　　I picked her up. "Where you going?" she asked me. "Going to MIT," I said, and a flirtation began. As we drew up to MIT, she said, "I'm going to a photography show. Would you like to come with me?" I said, "Why yes, I would love to go with you to a photography show."

　　　　At that moment, my memory of her disappears. I don't remember another word with her. I don't remember parking the car. I simply remember standing in front of a photograph. The photograph shocked me out of myself and literally made me dizzy, and I began to faint.

I had to grab on to the partition on which the photograph was mounted to steady myself. It was a feeling like the flu only magnified; that weakening of your body where you can't stand up and you've got a horrible flu. Your body is hot. It's cold. You're dizzy, and you can just barely hang on.

Peterson: It was physiological, in other words.

Weiss: I'm looking at this photograph, and in my heart I know that it's a fiction. It can't possibly be the truth of this world. Yet it was seamless, so at the same exact time, simultaneously, you had to believe it. Half of you said this is fraudulent. It's fake. The other half said it's got to be true. There it is. It's a photograph of the world, of the real world. Of course it's true. That duality knocked me out.

I remember leaving the show. It was called *Light Seven*, light to the seventh power, and on the way out I bought my first art catalogue. It cost three dollars. It was an Aperture monograph, the exhibition catalogue.

Peterson: That's a lot of bread back in the '60s.

Weiss: Yes. I took this catalogue home and went through it. It says, "Light Seven: Photographs from an Exhibition on a Theme. Edited by Minor White." I didn't know what a Minor White was. I didn't know if there was a major white, a medium white.

I looked him up in the phone book, found out we lived in the same town of Arlington, Massachusetts, called him up, and said, "I just saw this exhibit. I need to learn photography." His first words were, "Don't quit your job."

Peterson: Good advice.

Weiss: His next words were, "I think the best way to proceed would be to find someone to teach you at night." And he set me up with a teacher.

I'm a man with no mechanical aptitude and with a real fear of technical things. But I went out and bought all the photography stuff I needed the next Saturday. I said, "Sell me everything I need." They did. Got it home. Spread it all out on my bed, and I said, "Oh god, what have I done? What is all this stuff?"

There was an enlarger. A camera. There was film. There were canisters— aluminum cans of chemicals.

Peterson: All the stuff.

Weiss: I said, "I can't do this," but I did it anyway. I got some film in the camera, went out and shot, came back, mixed all the chemicals, somehow got the film on the reel, processed the stuff in my bathroom sink, and oh my god, I had negatives. I had negatives. Couldn't believe it.

Hung 'em out to dry, mixed the other chemicals, put them in black trays, put those black trays in the bathtub, set up my enlarger and put it on the end table, which I brought into the bathroom—hung a black cloth over the bathroom door, turned on the safe light. And they forgot to sell me a timer, so I used my wristwatch.

Peterson: I used to have a stopwatch draped over my neck.

Weiss: Got down on my knees—good metaphor—and stuck that piece of white paper into this black solution. It wasn't a white tray. It was a black tray.

Suddenly—this image appears. I said, "Oh my god. Oh my god, I gotta see this." Turned on the light, and the damned thing disappeared into blackness. *[laughter]* No stop, no fix.

Peterson: That brief shining moment.

Weiss: But I didn't care! I saw it. You know the feeling.

That feeling never leaves you, that feeling of amazement. In fact, tell me if this is true. We never quite knew why it worked. We just knew that if you stuck your paper, your light-sensitive paper, into this liquid, a picture would come up.

Peterson: The stripping away of this ion or that ion from a bunch of silver molecules. I knew how it behaved, that's about it.

John—I find your story unsatisfying in a certain respect. It's a beautiful story, but the way you talk about it—you describe that moment almost intellectually.

Weiss: I described my physical discomfort intellectually?

Peterson: Well, okay, that wasn't intellectual. I'll give you that, but no, the reason for it was a little bit too philosophical for my taste. In other words, well, there was this tension going on between illusion and reality . . .

Weiss: No, that's not what I meant to say. What I meant to say is it can't be true, but it is.

Peterson: Would any Jerry Uelsmann image have done that for you? Was there something specific about that picture that really knocked you on your ass? Jerry Uelsmann had a lot of pictures, you know.

I know that picture. You're looking up at this man standing on the earth, but the earth isn't the earth. There's rock. There's water, and then there's this weird thing above the guy that's like a tree, but what's it doing in the sky? Was there something about this particular picture that hit you on this mythological level?

Weiss: It's very hard for me to say exactly what it was that I felt. I can just tell you it upset me. It upset me because it said "this is true" and "this is fake" at the same time. That's what got me more than anything.

As I look at it now, I can say to you, yes, this guy in the picture is in silhouette, and he doesn't realize he's in peril, not to the degree that he should. There is something that seems evil to me floating over his head, a bush that's been ripped out of the earth and is now floating in the sky.

Peterson: He's facing the sky.

Weiss: No, he's looking forward. He doesn't see it. He doesn't know it's there, and it's hovering in a way that suggests something evil could happen.

Peterson: The man has no face. He's anonymous.

Weiss: That's right. His face is silhouetted. The man is closed down. The rock that he's standing on, the bush with the roots in the sky, it's all black. The sky is threatening. It is a dangerous picture.

Peterson: It's kind of ecstatic at the same time.

Weiss: It could be that he's climbed to the top of the world.

Peterson: Maybe you shouldn't read too much into it. I don't know. But there were years and years of living that led up to that moment. In other words, that moment was the beginning of something, and it was the end of something.

Weiss: What's interesting, Bri, is that I went from team sports to that singular activity, where there's no team. It's just you and your work.

It's private, man. You do it on your own. No one has asked you to do it. In fact, most people don't care you're doing it. In fact, no one cares you're doing it. No one cares, but you have to do it. It's your passion.

Peterson: Now, just one more question on this and then we drop it. What do you think would have happened if you had seen that Jerry Uelsmann picture, say, right after you left the baseball team?

Weiss: Nothing. I wouldn't have been ready for it.

Peterson: That's what I'm trying to get at. There's some kind of process involved where you had to drift for a while until you became desperate, though you didn't know it. You didn't even know you were unhappy.

Weiss: No, I knew I was unhappy.

Peterson: Okay, you knew you were unhappy, but you probably didn't know how unhappy.

Weiss: I didn't know how desperate I was.

Peterson: What I'm getting at is there was a hunger—you had this hunger, but you didn't even know you had the hunger. You would not have had the physiological response that you did if there wasn't something deep being activated at that moment.

Very few people have a straight-and-narrow path where they say, "Oh, I'm gonna be an artist." Then they get their résumé, and they get their job. Most people, if what they get is worth having, then there are a lot of dues to pay.

Everybody's story is different, but what if you hadn't listened? What would have happened to you if you wouldn't have seized that moment, if you wouldn't have been ready for it?

Weiss: You said everything was bringing me to that moment. It was waiting for me. Everything I was had prepared me to be ready, so if that moment hadn't appeared, we'll say for the sake of argument, if we follow your train of thought, that something else would have appeared, and I would have been a great haberdasher.

Peterson: You would have been a *dashing* haberdasher!

I'm saying it's possible to not be open to those moments. The cards are there, but you don't know how to pick 'em up and play. There's a drama unfolding and you can screw it up. You can make serious mistakes and not be open and not listen.

Then you get these people in their forties and fifties who are deeply unhappy. I'm really talking about myself if certain things hadn't happened the way they did for me, I could have lived a life that was conventional. Not this solitary journey we're talking about. Oh god, I would have been a horribly unhappy human being, just horribly, horribly.

I look at the boy/man who I was in those years, and I bow down to that kid. I'm grateful to that kid. He—had the—what, just the sense of adventure about life to say there's this thing I'm cut out to do, and I want that thing. Nobody's gonna stop me. I'm gonna get that thing.

Weiss: Well, you can say that now, but I read your book. There was a time when you were stopped and you couldn't do it, and you had no hope of doing it, and you went under.

Peterson: Pretty much, yeah. That's right. As it turned out, that was my bank experience. That was preparing the way.

Weiss: I don't talk about this a lot. First of all, the days of Minor White are long gone, but there was a time when his name was uppermost in everyone's mind in photography. There were those to whom he was beloved, to whom he was a father, to whom he was a guru. There were others who detested him and found him to be fraudulent and pompous, and silly, and they despised him, but his name was uppermost on the list of photographers because he was a photographer, and he was a teacher, and he was a writer, and he was a publisher.

Peterson: He was a force, yeah.

Weiss: He surrounded photography just when photography was being born as an art form. I didn't wanna trade on it—I wanted to be known for who I was and not for who I knew—and secondly, the more often I talk about it, the less special, it seems to me, it becomes.

I've told you stories within the past year or so that you had never heard before, and we've known each other since what year—'82? So over twenty years, about twenty-five years.

Peterson: We're pushing thirty, dude.

Weiss: Well, I'm saying, last year I think I told you over the phone one night part of the story I'm telling now.

Peterson: I'd never heard all of it before.

Weiss: That's why. Every once in a while, I'll let it out, but it's a conscious decision not to trade on it and not to let it drip away so that it becomes pedestrian. "Well, hi, I'm John. I grew up here. I went there. I did this. I did that."

Peterson: You're smarter than me 'cause I wrote a book about mine. What an idiot. *[laughter]*

Weiss: Give me the chance, buddy. I'd take it all back and put it out in a book.

Peterson: I hear you, John.

Weiss: It's like the lightning bolt pierced my heart, and so what am I gonna do? You can't ignore it. I was all in. All the chips I had left, all the chips I could imagine ever collecting, I put in. I put them in, and I knew it was right. I couldn't have explained it.

   The people in my life, family, said, "You are one stupid SOB. You failed at this. Now you're gonna fail at that, and nobody will ever hire you again." I thought to myself, "Could be. But I have no choice. I gotta do it."

   It wasn't just the thunderbolt and the lightning stroke. It was a human act of decision that came out of me, out of my soul. After all this stuff had impacted me, I had to make a choice. Do I dare, or do I not dare? Do I have the guts, or do I not have the guts?

   That was thrilling for me, and despite my family's very strong negative response, I did it. Oh, man, I was born in Boston at the age of twenty-eight. I literally was born that day.

Peterson: I can't add anything to that.

Weiss: You can understand this. There's never been a day since that I haven't loved photography with all my heart and honored it with all my humanity. I'm sitting here thinking right now, "Here we are talking, and I'm enjoying this. But I kinda feel the urge to go make a print."

Peterson: What gets my blood moving is just hearing the reality of the story, because it's your conversion, your Road to Damascus. I'm so intrigued by the connections between the spiritual call and the artistic call.

   I don't mean to gloss over the differences, but it reminds me of the Caravaggio painting of Saint Matthew where he's sitting there, just an ordinary guy, and the deity, in effect, strolls up, points at him, and says, "You, you, you're the one. Follow."

   His response is not, you know, the heavenly choirs start singing. It's more like, "Huh? Me? You gotta be kidding. I have a job. I gotta pay my rent." But he throws it all away and takes a chance.

   John. You almost fainted dead away, looking at that print.

Weiss: I did.

Peterson: How could you say no to that?

Weiss: Couldn't.

Peterson: You can't say no to that. To say no to that would be like saying, "I'll just go ahead and die now. I'm not gonna live a life worth living." To turn away from that call, I literally believe, is a kind of death. It would have been a death of your soul to do that.

Weiss: I think there are moments when we're really afraid. We're afraid of failure, or we're afraid of physical danger. Those moments are crystal clear in our minds. They never go away. This was a moment when I said yes. I was so afraid, but I said yes, and I'm proudest of that. I'm proudest of that. I said yes to life. I said yes to myself. I said yes to photography.

Peterson: And that's a scary moment.

Weiss: Scary 'cause I was jumping off a cliff. I was leaving a second job. I was newly married. I was gonna make a lot less money, and I was going to a place that was uncharted. I didn't know if I could do it.

Peterson: In other words, there was something about the "call" that said, what you were before isn't gonna work anymore. There's something new happening. Where you were was comfortable, and the call is pulling you out of that into some new thing.

It's exciting, but you don't know if you can do it. Almost every bone in your body is saying, "Oh, no, not me. I got this nice safe little life here. I got a roof over my head, and I'm paying my bills, and you want me to drop all that and become an artist? Are you kidding me?"

Weiss: The word *artist* never occurred to me. I'm a photographer.

Peterson: Sure, sure, I understand, we mean the same thing. But oh my god, the joy of that moment, 'cause you know you're alive. Whatever you are, you don't know, but you're pulled into life. You found your pathway, the thing that's gonna energize you from your molecules outward, and it's joyous. It's ecstatic.

I just think those moments are mysterious. Let's say this conversation gets published somewhere, and somebody reads it and says, "Hey, I want one of them moments too. That would be really cool. Maybe I'll go see a Jerry Uelsmann show and it'll happen to me."

The advice to that person is, forget about it. In other words, everybody's got their own story that they're living out. No one can live it for you. That's maybe the hardest thing about being an artist, when I finally realized that. I can study with people. I can study with John Weiss. I could study with Minor White. I can study with anybody. Ultimately it's not gonna help me. It'll help me just seeing how they did it, but no one can live my life for me.

That's the solitary thing we're talking about. As communal as it all is, it's you living your life, me living my life, and following the path that we need to follow. It's lonely and kinda scary. It's uncertain 'cause you can start down that path, and there's eight million ways you can mess it up. Nobody can tell you how to do it really.

That's the beauty of it too. That's what's so exciting about it. It's me living my life. I have a life. I'm living it as opposed to just drifting along. That's how I see your moment. It was a birth. You were born.

Weiss: That moment was kaleidoscopic. Looking back now, forty-two years later, you can examine it and come to terms with it and understand it. At the time, you're just living it and responding to it, and just somehow having the belief where you have no factual evidence, "I can do this. I have to try this. I got no choice. I've gotta do it."

To close yourself up and say no would have been a death.

Peterson: In fact, you're right. Talking about it dishonors it in a certain way. Once in a while, though, it's good to bring it into the light.

Weiss: You were talking about being on your own. I'm thinking now—you're talking to me as your teacher, and of course, you're my teacher as well, though you might not know it. Here's the thing. They give you courage. Teachers give you courage. You may be on your own. You may have your own path, but when things get tough, you've got that crutch of courage, knowing that someone else has done it, to lean on and to help you.

Peterson: So you know it's possible 'cause they did it.

Weiss: Once in a while, the teacher will come up to you, and in a metaphoric way, put his arm around you and say, "You got the guts, kid. You got the stuff. You can do it." We can't do it alone. We do the work alone, but I don't think we can do the work alone if we don't have that support somewhere.

Peterson: I think that's the best gift a teacher can give—not imparting knowledge per se, but just saying "I see something in you. Maybe even more than what you see. I see it, and I love what I see in you. You haven't really earned, frankly, my attention, because there's not much you have to give in return." In my case I knew it was true—there was nothing I had to offer my teachers, especially in the early years.

I was a messed-up, neurotic, misguided, lost, really damaged, wounded person. I really was. In retrospect, I look back at the amount of time and energy these guys gave me, and I think, what did they get out of it? It seemed totally one-sided. I got so much out of it myself.

They saw what I didn't see, which was some kind of hunger. There was something I wanted. I didn't know what it was, but they trusted my genuineness about it.

Weiss: They had a sense of you, your need, your humanity, your latent skills, whatever they were.

Peterson: I had no skills.

Weiss: Well, you did. You just didn't know what they were, but your teachers saw something in you that was worth investing in.

Peterson: I'm talking about even before I met you. One guy especially—this was a man toward the end of his career. After he retired, I went up to his house on Vancouver Island two or three times, and we talked all night. He had a big bay window looking out

BHP by JJ, February 4, 2015

across the bay toward the east. We would talk all night and then watch the sun come up in the morning.

Weiss: How cool is that?

Peterson: In other words, he gave me so much, and looking back on it I think, it was so one-sided, but—that's enough. I'm getting tired.

Weiss: One more thing: we both have been self-conscious at times, in the words that we were saying, as if to modify them and to edit ourselves. I called myself arrogant a few times.

Peterson: I called you arrogant.

Weiss: Yes, I enjoyed that. That I accept. I'm sitting here editing myself when in fact you and I have known each other for so long, and I can just say what's in my heart and know that you'll hear me. Right now I'm gonna stop editing myself. I'm gonna stop saying things to modify the truth of what's in my heart, and I'm just gonna say it. I'm just gonna be blunt and open and honest and let it come out however it wants to come out.

Peterson: What I'm saying now is, I'm gonna have some lunch, dude.

Weiss: Let's eat.

JJ by BHP, with additional JJ modifications. February 4, 2015

We made these pictures in John's house, goofing around after another conversation. He was moving to California a few days later, and I had the feeling that this was the last time I would see him. He died on May 27, 2017. In one of his last e-mails, he said, "If your new book reaches even one person, you've achieved a state of grace. So put it in the pond and let the ripples do their work." BHP

Eyes Wide Open

Eulogy delivered at the memorial service for Edward J. Sozanski, art critic for the
The Philadelphia Inquirer, *First Unitarian Church of Philadelphia, May 31, 2014*

The Sozanski giveth, the Sozanski taketh away—blessed be the name of Sozanski.

It embarrasses me now, but that used to be my standard "laugh line" at the Michener when we heard that the *Inquirer* art critic was paying us a visit. We knew we'd be in the spotlight, especially if we were scheduled for a review in the Sunday paper. For a small and insignificant institution in Doylestown, Pennsylvania, trying to establish itself in the public eye, desperate to be taken seriously, a visit by Ed Sozanski was a big deal.

I found out later that one of Ed's peculiar charms—in addition to grumpiness at actually having to endure groups of schoolchildren in museum galleries—was that he refused to think of himself as an influential person in the arts community. Some people in his position might have relished, even flaunted that prominence. To Ed, notoriety was more like one of those laser beams that artillery spotters use to paint their targets.

When I was nearing retirement, and both Ed and I had decided that friendship and ethics were reasonably compatible, I invited him to my sixtieth birthday party, along with a small group of friends. I was pleased to observe that he enjoyed himself and, despite his curmudgeonly reputation, even smiled occasionally. But he still seemed a bit uncomfortable, and at one point he took me aside and asked me to remind him of the names of a couple of the artists who were there. "Did I write about that one?" he mused aloud. My first thought was, he wants to know if he should put on his flak jacket. But it turned out that he was wondering if he might have hurt my feelings by saying something negative about one of my friends. What a burden this job was for him!

But also—and I know this seems an unlikely word for Ed—what a joy. This man enjoyed his work. Like all good writers, he loved words—the sounds, the rhythms—how he could use words not only as vehicles for thought but to seduce and caress or, depending on his mood, thrust and bludgeon. Sometimes he sounded like a delighted child. Sometimes—curators beware—he became a relentlessly clever and focused holy warrior of a wordsmith. When Ed decided he didn't like something—which usually meant a gap between intention and reality, or worse, when intention was so impoverished that the entire enterprise was dead in the water—well, he wielded a terrible swift sword indeed. I thought of Ed as the George Bernard Shaw of Broad Street. I don't make that comparison lightly. He had the necessary linguistic skills, but even more, the relentless intellect and go-for-the-jugular affability that were the renowned Englishman's trademarks. George Bernard Shaw meets the Energizer Bunny: that was Ed on a roll. He just kept going and going and going, finding endlessly interesting ways to say the same thing: the emperor has no clothes.

Problem was, I usually thought he was right, even when I was on the receiving end. My only criticism of the critic was that he would have benefited from spending a day or two in the shoes of the poor slobs whose job is not only to provide a nourishing meal to our customers but keep the doors open and pay the electric bills. When I mentioned this to Ed, he grunted. And in that grunt was all the reply he needed to make. "Maybe so," said the grunt. "But somebody has to keep you honest."

Early on I observed how seriously Ed took the issue of ethical conflicts and inappropriate influence. A certain mover and shaker in the art world was often seen at press conferences and receptions—always dressed impeccably, always working the room—the kind of person who'd mastered the art of the furtive glance at the name tag, and should the target not be worthy of attention, quickly moved on to greener pastures. Once at a press preview, while Ed was taking notes in the gallery no less, said personage showed up yet again and proceeded to turn on the charm. Ed listened politely, but soon raised an eyebrow and said drily, "You go to a lot of these things, don't you." His message was clear. I see you, he was saying, for the insincere flatterer you are. *So cease and desist.* With Ed, you harmed your cause by thinking he could possibly be influenced by anything, but especially a trivial conversation over a glass of sour Pinot Noir.

That was a window into the soul of this Sozanski fella, and I resolved at that moment to avoid him as if he were a cross between a flea and a tick respectively harboring bubonic plague and Lyme disease. He probably covered dozens of projects I authored, wearing both my artist and curator hats, and basically we never spoke. You want your space, I give you your space, was my silent mantra.

But, confession time—oh boy, did I look forward with anticipation and dread when I knew he'd made his visit, taken his notes, checked his facts, and then the day arrived. For the Sunday paper, I learned that the early edition showed up at the Wawa around noon on Saturday. I'd sit in my car, thumbing through the various sections, past business, past sports—but automotive was too far. There it was. He often mentioned curators by name—was I the hero or the goat? Either way, I knew I could count on that same gritty honesty, and a sense that he was like a sculptor who knew that a form existed in the stone, and every week he shaved a fleck or two off the marble.

Our friendship began slowly, when he wrote about my first memoir. Finally we could no longer avoid each other. What began as a standard phone interview—which curators learn to do while folding paper airplanes and tossing them at passing registrars—became a long, involved conversation about a hundred things that were really one thing. This crazy little thing called art.

Why do we do it, and once done, why do we need to, you know, figure it out? Why do certain quixotic fools persist in the conviction that art should speak to the lives and concerns of the moment, but also reach toward something more fundamental, something Duke Ellington called "beyond category," something that William Butler Yeats said, "thinks in a marrow bone."

Not that either one of us had any illusions about having all the answers. But Ed and I seemed to share something, The search, I guess. We called it applesauce. What we did—the thinking and the writing. Applesauce. I don't remember how it began, but before long Ed began to sign his e-mails "Johnny" (as in Appleseed), and he even gave me a book about the actual guy—Johnny Appleseed—which of course I never read. If I wanted to get a grin out of him, I'd ask, "How's the applesauce today, Jonny? Fresh Granny Smiths, or maybe a few sour Macintoshes thrown in?" Fine, he'd say, *except they keep giving me a smaller pot.*

Writers want more space for their words the way children want more marbles in their sandbox. But Ed's anger about his shrinking column was not garden-variety narcissism. The "Twitterization" of America had invaded his temple of words, and he was angry—not with his beloved editor, Becky, but with the higher-ups, the bean counters. This was his endless, and increasingly bitter, complaint—"eight hundred words." I can hear him say it as if each syllable were a piece of shrapnel between his teeth.

So when I woke up that terrible morning, saw a sympathetic e-mail from a friend, and opened the Kindle app on my iPad, as usual the first thing I saw was the word count. I chuckled, and the more I thought about it, the harder I laughed. "Well, Ed, at least you got twelve hundred words for your obit!"

I've learned what death feels like with someone I know well, like a mother, a father, a sister. When Ed died, it was a different kind of loss—someone whom I'd known as an abstraction, whose name I preceded with "the" and made jokes about his godlike stature, who had become a friend, but an unexplored friendship, a friendship hampered by thirty-some years of avoiding each other because we were each doing our jobs the way we believed they should be done. A friendship whose time ran out. We had talked longingly about sitting on my back porch, chatting all afternoon about whatever came up, with no worries about our jobs getting in the way. Finally, after I retired, we scheduled it—that long-delayed back porch conversation—but he couldn't get out of his driveway because of the ice, and then more time went by, and I was busy, and finally I wrote him to reschedule, and instead of writing back he up and croaked on me. The nerve of the old coot.

EJS and BHP at the Berman Museum of Art, January 30, 2014

The last time I saw him was over dinner, a few weeks earlier, with our respective soul mates there too. Surrounded by old movie posters, chattering TVs, and head shots of long-forgotten starlets, the four of us had a great conversation—lively, sharp, clever at times, always serious, never too serious. But Ed seemed vulnerable that night, quieter than usual, reflective.

We got to talking about a quality of character, of singularity, in the art we loved, more than surface beauty and style—that ancient need for the individual soul to make its mark, a quality that had always been elusive but perhaps was even harder to find now. I climbed on the soapbox and said that maybe, as a culture, we have made art too complicated—that I'd once heard the great choral conductor Robert Shaw describe the Brahms Requiem as "the last refuge of honor"— and that he was talking about a sense of deep honesty in Brahms. Brahms's music means what it says and says what it means. It's rooted in simple folk tunes, and despite vast sophistication of structure and language, it is still talking about things that pretty much everyone has a fair shot at understanding. Basic stuff like, we all are born, we all die, and we all struggle to do our best and often fail, but still we try to find meaning and beauty in our lives, and art needs to, somehow, add its voice to this search.

When I finished my speech and climbed off the soapbox, I glanced at Ed. The Sozanski mask—that tough, grim, skeptical visage—was melting away. He looked down, then up, made contact, looked down again, and then forward, directly at me, focused, with a sad, sweet smile and an unfamiliar mistiness in his eyes. He was no longer "the Sozanski." I was no longer "the museum curator." We were people who loved words—but now there were no words, just two simple suffering souls, sitting across from each other over a hamburger and a salad, trying to connect the dots.

Even now, I'm not sure why, but for a few precious seconds he opened the door of his house and ushered me in. Ed Sozanski—the warrior wordsmith, the George Bernard Shaw of Broad Street—finally revealed the soft, sweet, core of the cactus that the sharp spines protected.

That's the man I wish I'd known better. The man who was concerned about the effect of his words on others, but would not let that stop him from saying what he had to say. The man to whom ethics were not an abstraction but a way of life rooted in compassion and honesty. From that honesty grew stubborn idealism. Words must *mean* something and art must say something. And from that idealism grew the struggle for *clarity*. The need to see, and the need to help *us* see, clearly. See the difference between the cheap imitation and the real thing.

Ed Sozanski: eyes wide open. I can think of no better epitaph. And yes, to Ed, it was all simmering in the same pot: compassion, clarity, idealism, honesty. The best thing we can do to pay homage to his life and memory is to keep that same flame lit on our own proverbial stoves.

So thank you, Edward J. Sozanski, *Inquirer* art critic, for a lifetime of very fine applesauce—and thank you for letting me see, however briefly, a glimpse of the man behind the mask, the vulnerable, caring, heart of gold beneath that grumpy, crusty exterior.

I can hear the expressive grunt again, this time saying with a dry Sozanski twinkle, Can't you conjure up something better than that tired old cliché?

Sorry, my friend. We're all entitled to a juicy cliché once in a while. Crusty exterior—heart of gold. Works for me, Johnny. Works for me.

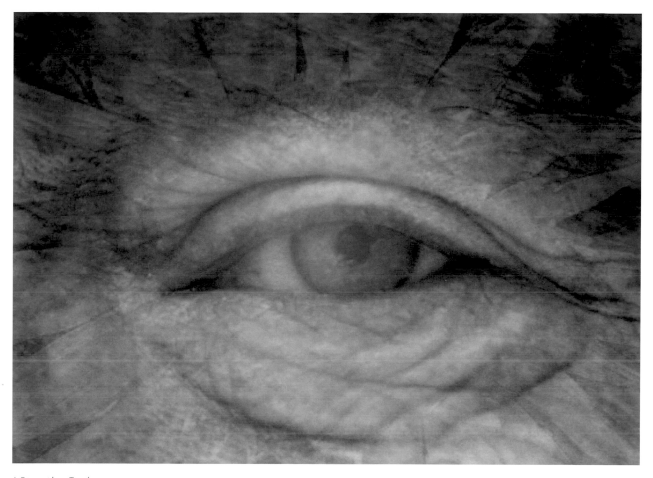

I Sing the Body #7, 2006

Wish You Were Here

Words of farewell to the Michener Art Museum on the occasion of the dedication
of the Brian H. Peterson Library and Research Center, June 9, 2014

They had chosen a good spot for their party. The trail meandered through the woods for a mile or two, then suddenly headed down to the creek, and they'd gathered together just where the view was the most spectacular. I had stopped there many times myself, pausing to take in the sunlight filtering through maples and oaks, and admiring the glowing hills on the other side of the valley below.

"So what are these idiots doing here?" I muttered to myself, observing their well-stocked coolers and picnic baskets. How dare they interrupt my precious solitude! I planned to simply walk by, communicating my displeasure with icy silence. But one of them called out to me. "Hey, you feel like joining us? We'd really appreciate it." There was something about the way he asked that got my attention.

So I rested for a few minutes and heard their story. They had gathered there to honor the memory of a friend who had recently died. He was way too young and way too nice for such a terrible fate, and they'd wracked their brains to figure out the best way to remember him. Finally they decided to pool their resources and buy one of those commemorative benches. Then they had to figure out where to put it, and settled on this spot. "It was his favorite place in the world," one of them said.

The party had been planned months earlier, but naturally, this being Philadelphia, the bench wasn't finished. They had the party anyway.

I wondered if I might have run into him, on one walk or another. They showed me his picture. Nope.

A dead guy whom I'd never met. But he was a kindred spirit. Even more, I was moved by the kindness of his friends. They had decided to share this moment with anyone who happened to walk by, because that was what they'd learned from the life of their comrade. Generosity. What's the point of having something, seeing something, knowing something, if you keep it to yourself?

I didn't want to linger, so I thanked them and took off. As I walked down the trail toward the creek, I barely noticed how stirred up I was inside, until I instinctively raised my hand and brushed the wet place on my cheek.

Some weeks later the bench finally appeared. I'd been wondering what words they would put on the little brass plate. To my surprise, there were no colorful remembrances, no over-the-top descriptions of their friend. Not even his name. Just four simple words: "Wish you were here."

Since that day I've had plenty of opportunities to think about why those good people chose *those* words for their friend's bench.

Wish you were here. When you reach a certain age, the list of people for whom those sentiments apply is like the credits of a movie. Think the opening minutes of *Star Wars*: a dismal succession of names that stretches out to infinity—a style of credits, by the way, that the video editing software in my laptop calls "Far Far Away."

Ain't that the truth—far, far away! When someone takes off for the Great Beyond, or wherever we go or don't go when the jig is up—well, to restate the obvious, they're not just far, far away—they be vanished, expired, up in smoke, *finito la musica*.

For all the mountains we climb, all the buildings we build, all the worthy stuff we create, is there anything more important than the friends we make, the family we love, the connections we form with the people of this earth? Not "the people" as in nations and cultures, but the flesh-and-blood Toms, Janes, and Sherries who love us and care about who we are?

When these people start to go, they leave holes in our lives. Big holes that the passage of time smooths out and rounds off, but never fills in.

Which brings me to another subject: granite. Or perhaps brass, or fired clay, or vinyl letters, or one of those hard-to-read wall labels in a museum.

When people go away, we need to remember them. Heck, we even need to remember them *before* they go away, because we know they will go away, and it's good to tell them that they matter to us while they're still here.

In the twenty-four years that I worked at the Michener, the place gradually filled up with markers, plaques, and monuments of various kinds. I saw them on the walls of galleries announcing that this room is named after so-and-so. I saw them on bricks and benches, on doorways and in hallways, and I always reminded myself how important they are to the institution—how much we were able to accomplish because putting a name on a plaque is something that matters to people.

I must confess that in my heart of hearts, this "naming" of things used to strike me as empty calories. I was grateful for it, I respected the people who do it, but to paraphrase Shakespeare, a gallery by any other name would have just as many pretty landscapes on its walls.

Then I began to think about all the empty places in *my* life . . .

My parents were children of the Depression. They valued education because they both had to fight for it themselves. First my mother had to rebel against her own mother, who said that college was out of the question and the best path for a woman was to learn how to type. Then, after the war, Mom had to endure plenty of raised eyebrows when she put her youngest child—me—in day care so she could finally finish her degree. What people didn't know was that she was also teaching me how to read by pointing out words in *Time* magazine while I sat on her lap. For twenty-five years Mom braved the Montana winters to get to her teaching job on time.

My father gave up a full college scholarship and worked as a butcher to help his family during the Depression. He got his education largely through the G.I. Bill after the war, and had a distinguished career as a geologist. His own father, my grandfather, lost the family farm to foreclosure in the thirties and spent the rest of his working years as a laborer, mostly a night watchman in a boiler factory. The constant noise made him completely deaf, and the only way he could communicate was to pass notes back and forth. After he retired, he began to visit the local library. His days on earth were nearly over just when he began to discover his true passion: the world of books and knowledge. One of the last things he said to his son, my father, was "I feel cheated." I wonder what my grandfather would have said had he known that his grandson's name would grace a museum library.

After all these years, I've learned that an institution like ours is built on the same feelings those people I met in the park felt thirty-some years ago.

I want to remember. I want to be remembered. And I want to say thank-you to people I care about, who cared about me. What could be more basic?

It doesn't matter that to everyone else they're just names on a wall. To those who knew them, the names were flesh-and-blood people who, in a way, are still here—in shared places, objects, stories. *They are the soil from which we grew.*

I see it now, finally. I thought we were building a museum out of paintings and sculptures. But the bricks and mortar of a museum are also made of love, loss, memory, and gratitude.

So I am honored to take my place among those names. And especially happy to be haunting the library with my dear friend Evelyn Fairstone, the Michener's first volunteer and archivist, who gave a good part of her life to creating and maintaining the library, and whose picture is just inside the door. Evelyn suffered much, including losing several family members who died in the

Holocaust, yet she was the kindest and sweetest soul who ever walked this earth. Every Monday morning I'd drop by the library and get my Evelyn hug and start the week with a smile.

I've heard myself described as the soul of the Michener, and while I was flattered, I knew that honor really belonged to Evelyn. Evelyn understood that a museum is about service to a higher cause and is a symbol of knowledge and the search for truth. Simply by being the generous person she was, Evelyn reminded me why I got into museum work and what I hope to leave behind. I look back at my career, and think of those people I met in the woods thirty years ago, and you know—I was just a guy inviting people to the picnic. Every exhibition, every lecture, every docent talk, every tour—that was me saying, *Come on over here, friend, share the food and drink, and help us remember what really matters.*

Generosity. What's the point of having something, seeing something, knowing something, if you keep it to yourself? Museums are about the seeing and the knowing, but mostly, museums are about giving to others what's seen and known.

Bruce Katsiff, my former boss whose belief in my ability opened the door to this adventure, used to tease me about long-winded curators by quoting Evan Turner, a famous museum director. "Hey Bri," Bruce would say, "Evan Turner told his curators that the Lord's Prayer is only seventy-five words. Why do you need three hundred for a text panel?" To which I'd reply, "Fine, but look who wrote those seventy-five words. That's some heavy competition."

Okay, bring it on—Bruce, I'll take your challenge and wrap the whole thing up with a dozen words: "Blessed are the hungry, for they shall be invited to the picnic." Thank you for coming to the picnic. Thank you for inviting me to *your* picnic. And thank you for being hungry, because hunger, yours and mine, has kept me honest. And especially, thank you, to my shipmate and soul mate, my wife, Helen, who has had my back, been by my side, through thick and thin, good and bad, ups and downs, who has endured my tantrums and shared my joy.

When my mother died a few years ago, my brother and I found a huge folder of articles and reviews she'd saved that documented my work at the museum. My parents, my grandparents, who had to struggle for what my generation so takes for granted, would be proud of this moment. Proud that their son and their grandson will be remembered in this place of life, hope, creativity, and beauty that he helped to build.

So when you see those signs on the walls filled with names of people you never knew, think of that picnic in the woods, look around at the nourishing stuff on the picnic table, and remember all the people who gave of themselves so that you could be standing in this beautiful place, enjoying the meal. And then remember those four little words inscribed on the park bench: Wish you were here. Wish you were here.

Thank you, and safe journey.

Helen and BHP, leaving the Michener after the dedication ceremony,
June 9, 2014. Photograph by Tom Shillea.

Conversation: As Beautiful As . . .

Standing in front of the class, I had the best view in the room, and it was beautiful. The delicate dance of love, performed week by week before my eyes, as I pumped their heads full of f-stops and focal lengths, formalism and photo essays. It began with glances, a few shared words, smiles back and forth. Soon they were walking in the room together at the beginning of class, sitting next to each other, holding hands and whispering during my brilliant critiques. Young love, blossoming in Photography 101, under my watchful eye. I felt responsible, protective, as if my words somehow helped the process along, and I told my friends that I was finally an official teacher because two people had fallen in love in my classroom.

As a teacher I was connecting with people every day, and for a moment in their lives that connection had an effect, an influence, impossible to measure but real. This soul-to-soul connection disappeared when I became a curator, and I missed it. You put the shows together, slap 'em on the walls, then go back to your office and get busy with the next one. Sure, there were gallery talks and reviews and lectures, but rarely a sense of comradeship, of shared journey.

As years and shows flowed by, I tinkered with ways to get a conversation going with my "customers" but was never satisfied with the results. The truth is, I wasn't ready myself to take the necessary leap into the unknown. It's hard to make complex ideas user-friendly—even harder to write conversational prose that's also serious and purposeful. Took me nearly twenty tears to get the confidence and clout to actually do it.

The "beauty show" at the Michener Art Museum began as a reaction to criticism from a major foundation that our exhibit program lacked "artistic quality" because it was too conventional, not avant-garde enough, not experimental, not hip or trendy or cool enough. The fact that we were fabulously successful and had made a long series of intelligent decisions to get there didn't matter to the foundation, nor did the effect that a steady diet of hard core avant-garde stuff would have on our attendance.

In a fit of pique I asked myself what exhibit idea would be most guaranteed to annoy those pushy funders who thought they were so smart. How about a show on beauty? One that was not ironic or did not trivialize the idea by reducing it to an illusion of culture or a subjective, "eye of the beholder" thing. An exhibit that honored beauty, explored it through actual work by actual living artists (poets and photographers), and respected its complexity and contradictions.

The exhibition included several opportunities for audience participation, including one that asked the visitor to finish the phrase, "As beautiful as . . ." The responses flowed to my desk once a week, and each time they arrived, I was more amazed. They were clever, well spoken, courageous and inventive and thoughtful. And they were perfectly in tune with the complex and contradictory experience of beauty I was trying to share. All these people—I had no idea who they were, where they came from, or any other demographics except they were human organisms who happened to see the show and they got it. They understood. We had connected, more perfectly than I could have ever hoped.

Were I to take on the job of making my own "As beautiful as . . ." list, this is where I'd start, because it's beautiful how an exhibition I dreamed up for such terrible reasons initially could end up stimulating such a meaningful conversation.

Perhaps the best way to say thanks to these people would be to share their wisdom with others of like mind. Some of my favorites of these mighty morsels follow, preceded by a few excerpts from the exhibit script to give some context. I wrote the script but claim no authorship of the rest, other than creating a stage where the story could unfold.

Making Magic: Beauty in Word and Image
James A. Michener Art Museum
November 3, 2012—March 31, 2013

Excerpts from the catalogue and exhibit script:

Much has been said about what defines us as a species—what "makes us human." Many years ago I stumbled on a possible answer to this question in a book by a famous archaeologist whose name I've forgotten. The great scientist suddenly took off his lab coat and imagined what it was like to be one of the people he'd been studying. Why did our ancient ancestor choose to make his spear points on a hill overlooking a peaceful valley? Was it simply to scout for the next herd of woolly mammoths, or because he enjoyed the view? And why did this "caveman" make such elegantly designed objects? Why the attention to detail, the unnecessary decorations? Why were the tools so beautiful?

If you're curious about what makes us who we are, then imagine a world in which all created things do nothing more than perform a function. Imagine a world without beauty.

Beauty. It's all around us, everywhere, but when you try to pin it down, it slips through your fingers. Like a mosquito dive-bombing your ears—you know it's there but you can never quite catch up to it. Maybe you'll even stop to admire the corpuscle thief when it finally lands on your arm—before you flatten it with a bloody, satisfying splat.

Take a look at a mosquito sometime, if you dare. What a beautiful bug! So fragile, so delicate as it descends, slowly, steadily, proboscis extended, light as a dandelion seed riding the wind. Beautiful—and dangerous. When it bites, you'll be scratching that itch for a very long time. . . .

I don't expect you to agree with me about this elusive phenomenon. You may, in fact, believe that mosquitos are ugly, and anyone who disagrees need only look at the welt on one's arm and think about encephalitis.

The world has an endless capacity for terror, and an infinite supply of beauty. Beauty and terror are woven together in every moment of our lives. Beauty is not a vacation from reality. It is reality.

Visitors respond: How do you experience beauty in your own life? Please finish the following sentence, and your response may become part of the exhibition.

"As beautiful as ... "

The color of marigolds.

Returning to my homeland after not seeing my family for over twenty years.

The first cry of a newborn baby.

The morning fog on a mountain lake.

Seeing someone help an injured animal.

A brand new hardcover book (no dustcover needed) and a satin bookmark.

A shining pearl of dew on a blade of grass.

A ride on the carousel with my mother when I was five years old.

Lying under trees, watching their leaves shift and tremble, their colors and the sunshine and shade, moving, moving, moving, pulling me up toward them.

A family of wild turkeys walking together by the lake.

A freshly washed blackboard on Fridays at school.

The endless sea.

Crying helplessly over the ending to a book that has become a companion.

The feeling of being loved.

New York City at night.

Choosing to do what is right.

Flying in an open cockpit plane above the Delaware River.

Watching my babies grow to be kind people.

Discovering new lines on the faces of my parents each time I see them.

A baby's hand reaching out to touch her mother's face.

The wails of a grieving woman after losing her beloved husband.

A cat napping in the sun.

Watching an elderly parent pass on.

Doing my first back handspring!

The man I love reaching for my hand to keep me from falling in the stream.

The fireflies dancing over a field in the purple twilight of summer.

Letting go of anger and experiencing a feeling of forgiveness.

The realization of how we are all perfect and imperfect—different and the same.

The light God created before he created the sun.

Sitting in a field, looking up at the stars.

My grandson, twelve hours old, when he met and held my gaze, his dark eyes taking everything in. My heart overflowed with peace and joy; I knew eternity.

Understanding how something is made.

Opening a new pack of my favorite brand of pens. It's the little things . . .

Discovering just how far I have come.

Feeling the infinity of a second.

The smell of my infant daughter. The softness of her skin. The shape of her rosebud lips. The pressure of her tiny fingers on my face.

Living with my wife.

Sitting in my friend's kitchen this morning drinking coffee and seeing her frailty but trusting I could touch her knee and it would comfort her.

My mother blasting a Talking Heads record and dancing with her eyes closed.

The world.

A song.

Scratching where I itch.

Silence.

Peace.

Forest Light #14, 1992

A Journey Worth Taking

Book review: *Exhibit Labels: An Interpretive Approach, Second Edition*, by Beverly Serrell. Published by Rowman & Littlefield, 2015. 376 pages. [This article first appeared in *Exhibition* (spring 2016), vol. 35, no. 1, and is reproduced with permission.]

I was halfway through the exhibition when it hit me: two parts disappointment and one part impatience, with a dash of resignation and a pinch of embarrassment.

The show was one of those extravaganzas that only big museums can pull off. There's usually a Birth or a Golden Age attached to an easily marketable idea, and the goal is to stuff the place with bona fide masterpieces that look great on membership envelopes and keep those turnstiles turning. It's a reliable formula that doesn't necessarily produce the most reliable scholarship. But the lights stay on and the doors open.

What incredible beasts of the painter's art were in that show: American, European, historic, modern, canvas after canvas, room after room. I felt like I'd never seen a painting before. I was absorbed, exhilarated, eager for more.

Excitement begat curiosity. Words, words, on the walls—a little help, please. Information is nice, but give me guidance, insight, the telling detail. Show me the power of the written word to remember and reveal. Remind me that when I'm hungry, a museum will always have something nourishing on the menu.

What did these labels offer? Mostly provenance. I say again. PROVENANCE. "This painting was owned by Countess Brunhilde the Fourth, then through the marriage of her son Prince Elvis of Macedonia in 1789 passed to the Duchess of Yorkshire for whom the Yorkshire Terrier was named …."

I wondered if these label writers, in a five-star restaurant, would ignore the filet mignon and gorge themselves on Grey Poupon. I remembered what a friend had said about museums, how they made her feel like the dumbest kid in Sunday school, and the text panels were "sermons."

A ton of bricks fell. *We have a problem.* What we do—we must do it better. And not just curators. The entire museum enterprise has a responsibility not only to preserve and understand but to communicate, to connect.

I've met many fine exhibit writers who've had similar epiphanies. Most are content with knowing the difference and doing good work. Beverly Serrell wrote a book. More like *the* book. For people who want to do it better, the source for practical wisdom has been her 1996 volume *Exhibit Writing: An Interpretive Approach.*

The museum world owes a great debt to Ms. Serrell for her disciplined, passionate advocacy of excellence in exhibit writing. She was an early voice for humanizing the museum experience, insisting that the anonymous, authoritative tone—what my friend called sermons—was downright unfriendly.

Serrell's core message: we can trust the essential humanity of our visitors, and if we search for common ground we'll probably find it. In the process, we'll form new friendships instead of making people feel stupid because they don't know the difference between a meerkat and a tomcat.

As Serrell puts it, "We must keep in mind the visitors' emotions, their yearning for continuity, love of a good story, ability to see and seek patterns, and natural spirituality."

Serrell addresses questions that every writer wrestles with: who's reading this, how long should it be, how complicated, how should it be structured? Her focus is on bringing the novice label writer to a level of basic literacy, as well as giving the complacent veteran a push in the right direction. She has found logical ways to divide her complex subject into its essential components, and has a gift for readable prose.

As a teacher, Serrell's style is reductionist and her tone, emphatic—*here's what the research says, these are the guidelines*. Lists, rules, and bullet points are common. She has the purposefulness of a crusader, and with all that data to back her up, who would argue with the rightness of her cause?

Exhibit writing lives in an environment not unlike a modern factory farm, where words are born and grow in a cruel box of restrictive parameters and "group think," then are processed and served as bland, generic McNuggets. Somehow, miraculously, good exhibit writers keep churning out good stuff, doing the impossible so smoothly that their virtuosity goes unnoticed.

Such skillful wordsmiths can be difficult to find, expensive, and a challenge to work with. Academically trained curators tend to write for each other, while educators and "hired gun" consultants have the creativity and basic language skills, but may lack the nuanced mastery of word and content that a fine-tuned label requires. And in smaller institutions, a label writer might also be docent, registrar, and occasional janitor.

Thus the need for Beverly Serrell's book. But in her relentless drive to raise standards lurks the danger of a new orthodoxy almost as worrisome as the lifeless, authoritative voice it replaces.

The prevailing ethos of Serrell's universe is Utilitarian, that is, the greatest good for the greatest number. Labels must be written at a 12th-grade level and no longer than 60 words because research proves that more visitors will read them. Yes, we *must* reach out to our visitors and the more the merrier. But is that the end or the beginning of the journey?

Exhibit writing is an art form as surely as Shakespeare's sonnets or Basho's haiku. If we strive for excellence, then let us not fear the truly excellent or delude ourselves into thinking we can get there in a few easy steps. One might follow every rule and incorporate every bit of wisdom that research provides, and the results could easily be formulaic and miss the mark by a mile.

Serrell's book will always have an honored place on my bookshelf. Like all technical manuals—and this is one of the best I've seen—it must be studied and digested, added to the internal toolkit, then forgotten in the joy of crafting sentences that sing, and in the deep satisfaction of finding the right word in the right place, for the right reasons.

It's possible to make memorable, life-affirming, even life-changing exhibitions that put words to work creatively. Many people will follow where we lead if we treat them with generosity and respect.

A more humanistic ethos has begun to flow through the museum community, thanks to dedicated, caring people like Beverly Serrell. My "provenance" experience is increasingly rare. Old school, autocratic curators who insist on what Serrell calls the "curatorial agenda" may soon find themselves in another line of work.

Yet one person's agenda is another's article of faith. Museums are educational institutions, and also seekers and bearers of truth, however that may be defined. Instead of seeing people as hostile "agendas," are we not better off looking for innovative ways to bring those competing voices together?

Mexican poet and essayist Octavio Paz points the way to a new—and ageless—definition of excellence in an essay on the "staying power" of poetry: "Rejecting the marketplace, costing almost nothing at all, it goes from mouth to mouth, like air and water."*

Sixty words, a hundred sixty, even, God forbid, sixteen hundred—the goal of pleasing the multitude always ends up at the one. You. Me. What moves us and connects us, what transforms our lives.

Words do that. The right ones, for the right reasons. Finding them is a journey worth taking.

*Octavio Paz, "Poetry and the Free Market," *New York Times Book Review*, December 8, 1991.

I Saw This #34, 2016

Generosity

It was three months from beginning to end. Roughly. I think the big family meeting was in early November. She died in late January.

The meeting was required by the hospice lady. I wish I could remember her name . . . Hispanic, midforties, short hair. Plump but not too plump. Posture: steady and straight. Eyes: focused, but open. Attentive. And sad. A cup of grief poured into a bowl of generosity, seasoned with kindness. And not afraid to talk about the rough stuff. Wish I could remember her name . . .

The hospice lady led the meeting. Wendy sat quietly and watched. It was odd for someone else to be in charge of things in my sister's house. But it had to be that way.

There would be the Hollywood version, and then there would be what actually happened. Hollywood—the dying person was patient and kind, the rest of us were caring and wise. We laughed, we cried, and topped it off with a big group hug. What really happened—the dying person was cranky and uncomfortable, we were frozen with dread and unable to process what was happening, and it ended with everybody kind of drifting away.

There were moments. My older nephew promised, with all the solemnity and seriousness he could muster, that he and his brother would always stay connected with her two teenage daughters. I admired him for that. Respected his bigheartedness. I could see that he believed this was the most important gift he could give her. But Wendy was too distracted, too caught up in her own pain and frustration to graciously accept what he was giving.

She said little when he'd finished speaking—and in her silence I felt a certain skepticism, a hint of "what's the big deal about that, you want a medal or something?" He felt it too, and his quiet anticipation turned into barely suppressed surprise and disappointment.

At least we were all in the room. That's my family—confused, often unhappy, with so much left unsaid—but there, in the building. My family shows up when it matters.

The hospice lady—I can see her so clearly, even though the rest of that day has faded. The way she scanned the room, took it in, understood, forgave. The dignity and simplicity of her words. I wondered what she'd seen, what she'd learned in all the other meetings like this one.

I know she came back a few times in the next three months, but I didn't see her again until the day after Wendy died. For some reason—and now, looking back, what a stupid idea—I stayed in Wendy's house that first night. By myself. There was some logic to it at the time—maybe somebody needed to be there in the morning, maybe there was a security issue. But nobody asked me to stay at the house, and one or two people tried to talk me out of it. So I have no one to blame but myself.

I needed to say good-bye, and that's what I did. I spent a couple hours just wandering through her house. I looked at her books—Russian novels, travel books, medical textbooks. I studied the pictures on her walls, including four or five that were *my* pictures, ones I'd given her for various birthdays over the years, and she'd actually hung them, in prominent places too. I noticed things that I'd never seen before—the beauty of the rugs she'd bought on her travels, the quirky humor in the knickknacks she'd picked up, the pictures on her fridge—all the minor details of a life lived, a life now over.

Other than memories and evidence of what I'd lost, my only companion that night was my sister's cat, who did his usual cat stuff, oblivious to how his life was about to change. He played with his ball of yarn, slept on his favorite pillow on the couch, and raced through the house in the middle of the night chasing phantom mice.

In the morning, as I was eating my cereal and reading the paper, the doorbell rang. It was the cleaning crew, all snappy and snazzy in their uniforms, ready for another battle in the war with cobwebs and dust. They'd been coming for years and expected to see Wendy at the door. Instead they saw me, a strange bearded fellow, no doubt dazed and bleary-eyed, who informed them that the person they knew was dead, but yes, they should still clean the house, but we'd be in touch because we weren't sure how much longer it would be necessary. The looks on their faces. They'd known that something was wrong, but not *that* wrong.

They were surprised, upset—but they did their jobs. And I started in on the phone calls—endless phone calls. My brother and I had divided these chores, which included canceling the cable and Internet, shutting off the electricity and phone, stopping various memberships and magazine subscriptions, calling the newspaper to place the obituary.

Somehow the hospice lady got a call through. She must have been persistent. The phone rang, I picked it up, and immediately I understood why she'd chosen to spend her time with dying people and the people who love dying people. Her voice was so clear, so caring—but simple. No pretense. She must have heard something in *my* voice, because she asked, "Are you okay? Do you want me to drop by?"

"Yes," I said. "If it's not too much trouble. Yes."

A few minutes later she was there. She sat next to me on the couch and asked me a few questions. I trusted her. And suddenly it all poured out. Everything. All the terror and horror of the previous three months, all the family craziness, all the good-byes to the books and the knickknacks and the cat. I sat on that couch and wept, without shame, without reservation, for at least an hour, and she listened, once in a while touching my hand, here and there asking another question, gently guiding me to the center of my hurt, helping me get comfortable with it, knowing that it would be my new home.

Meanwhile the cleaning crew ranged through the house with vacuums blaring and spray cans spraying. I saw the workers stare—discreetly—at the drama unfolding on the couch, but I didn't care. Nothing else mattered to me but the pain I felt and the need to release the pain into the universe.

I'm tempted to say, "That was the moment when . . ." or "After that day nothing was the same." But there was no summing up, no moment of being "over it." It was more like waves, cresting and crashing on the beach. With each wave I was back on that couch again, pulled inward, toward the hurt, but also pushed upward, into life. As the months flowed by, the jagged edges of the wound slowly smoothed out. But it's still there. Always will be.

In case you're wondering, I never saw her again. The hospice lady, I mean. Not sure I even spoke with her another time. Maybe I called her up just to let her know I was okay. Yes, it's coming back to me. I believe I did call her a day or two later, because it would have felt funny not to. She was gracious, but I could tell she had already moved on to the next one, the next person who needed help like I did. Like we all do.

Interior Light #12, 2003

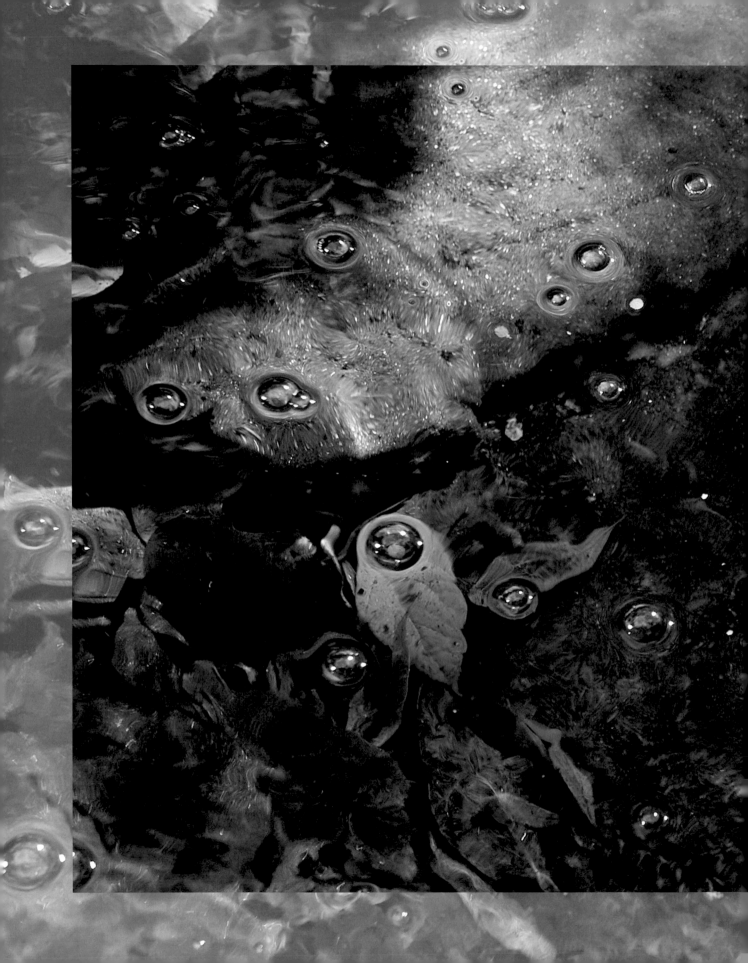

Alone

You know you need more dopamine when: you're glad to be using a walking stick because it means you're still walking.

I barely notice the tapping any more—the steady *thwip, thwap* of rubber tip on floor as I navigate my way through the house. Except when I'm in our kitchen, where the sound reverberates up from the linoleum and echoes briefly over the table before dissipating in midair, bouncing back and forth between engagements, marriages, grandchildren, vacations, ancestors, births.

My favorite photograph is the large black-and-white in a wood frame: smiling couple in windbreakers, standing next to each other on a bare rock, lake stretched out behind them, hair blowing wildly. I had ten seconds to get from camera to rock, pull her close, smile. The rock was steep, a bit slippery, but just a quick jump and a few big steps and I was by her side with my arm around her shoulder. Too far away to hear the click, but I could see the shutter open and close. Glad to have that picture. Not doing much rock climbing these days.

You know you need more dopamine when: not having brain surgery (too risky) is more terrifying than being awake while somebody drills holes in your skull.

Thwip, thwap. In most places no one pays much attention because they're too busy. But in restaurants, airports, lobbies—anywhere people have nothing to do but sit and wait—the calipers come out. Heads turn, brows furrow, eyes discretely glance in the direction of this old guy with the blazing white beard and ponytail, paunchy but solidly built, baseball cap and black walking stick with rubber grip, who moves so carefully between chair legs and doorways, stopping and starting, as if he's in an obstacle course instead of a diner or a dentist's office.

It must go back to some instinctive need to size people up—friend or foe, fight or flight, that sort of thing. Maybe there's a gene for it, because nearly everybody plays this game—I do too. I call it Name That Disorder. You see someone who has a problem, some odd behavior, a set of physical symptoms, and your brain starts to scan a taxonomic checklist, sorting through whatever scant knowledge you have about this or that, finally arriving at: (A) drunk; (B) mentally challenged; (C) knee or hip surgery; (D) neurological disorder that destroys dopaminergic neurons; (E) all of the above.

The problem is, even highly trained neuron docs don't have a surefire way of diagnosing Parkinson's disease, and sometimes people suffer for years before someone figures it out.

Those docs are pretty smart though. They told me early on that I have a subspecies that responds well to the drugs but progresses more quickly. I decided, however, that they were wrong. This wouldn't apply, you know, to me. I didn't realize I'd made this decision. I was just being the stubborn and delusional person I'm wired to be.

Several years and a couple doctors later, sitting on an examining table, I heard the words, "In a year or so you will need a cane or a walker, and a wheelchair's not far behind, and by the time you're sixty-five you won't be able to move around without assistance." I looked at my high-powered neurologist like he was saying palm trees grow at the North Pole.

I said, "If an act of will can at least slow this thing down, I'm your guy." He looked down at the floor, said nothing. The thing is, I am the perfect patient. A doctor told me that. For years I'd downed the right pills, seen the right doctors, read the right books. I knew more about Parkinson's disease than an average physician. Doctors asked me questions about how it's managed. Okay, that happened once. But still, it happened.

I'd bicepped and tricepped, gluted and hamstringed, pushed, pulled, squatted, stretched. Exercise, yes. But I'd hired personal trainers, twice a week, three times a week, costing me as much dough as a modest mortgage. I mean, these drill sergeants practically killed me some days. I told them to jack it up.

Thanks to the exercise, my suit jackets no longer fit me—had to buy new ones, a size or two larger. I was proud of it. People who hadn't seen me in a while would inevitably begin a conversation with "You look great!" I'd never cared about my body before. Not really.

Drugs. Exercise. Then there were the video games. Not the shoot-'em-up, destroy-all-zombies kind. I have a movement disorder—so I bought every system, every game that forced my legs and arms to move.

I did everything a human being could possibly do to beat back the wolves short of snake oil and green smoothies with magical healing powers.

But the wolves have nothing to prove. They take all the time they need. Wolves—no, that doesn't quite describe it; more like an army of invisible worms with teeth, patiently burrowing into soft, captive flesh, savoring every bite.

Friends tease me about the lengthy row of video game boxes below my TV. These so-called friends totally miss the point. I tell people I see a personal trainer twice a week, and if I say "she," they reply, "Oh really, a 'personal trainer,' eh?" As if the two words are synonymous with "hankie-pankie." These people haven't a clue.

It's hard, even, for my wife sometimes, the mate of my soul, who cares for me in ways too personal to share. And I can see it—the trainer and I interact physically, we talk, we share things, a bond forms, one thing leads to another—what wife wouldn't worry, just a little, about her husband in that situation? I can see it. Even she, who knows me better than anyone, who has seen me at my best and my worst, who would do anything to make my body behave—sometimes, once in a while, even she doesn't understand.

 I'm fighting for my life. You got that, people? My life. The wolves, the flesh-eating worms, the dopamine riff—those aren't just clever words on a page. Every breath, every heartbeat, every nanosecond that we have here—it's worth fighting for.

Now, as I tap my way around the house, and glance at the exercise equipment and the video game boxes, I see desperation. Desperate to finish what I started, and desperate to control what can't be controlled.

I take pride in self-knowledge—consider it the highest human achievement. Often it comes by living your illusions until reality reaches out and kicks you where it hurts.

I felt that kick when my legs stopped moving in the middle of a coffee shop one dark February night and I couldn't get them to start up again. The legs just wouldn't move. Another kick happened in an airport, when I got so frustrated with my body's refusal to cooperate that I gave in to my rage and decided to walk to the gate instead of riding the stupid golf cart, only to freeze up in a crowded hallway while Helen looked on in helpless horror.

And finally, in the middle of the night, in our small winter apartment, the moment arrived when I couldn't avoid the truth anymore, with my wife holding me in her arms, when all the years of studying my enemy and fighting and refusing to admit that this disease would have its way with me, it all came out in a rush and I broke down and wept like a motherless and fatherless child.

You know you need more dopamine when: the first thing you think about in a restaurant is how far your table will be from the bathroom.

A few days after my long overdue meltdown, I met an old friend for lunch. Sure enough, he'd arrived first and placed us at the most mathematically distant location possible from the WC. "Not letting a few lousy neurons ruin MY life," I muttered to myself as I tapped my way in his direction, lurching forward here and there, grabbing the back of a stranger's chair to prevent disaster, and every head in the room turned in my direction.

I think I'll have somebody make an LCD sign that I can wear on my back and turn on when necessary. PARKINSON'S DISEASE, the display will read, followed by RESUME YOUR LIVES NOW.

Halfway through lunch, the bladder spoke. I excused myself. My friend looked at me and said, "Will you be okay? Need some help?"

"Nope," I said, "Just get comfortable."

Turned out that half the restaurant was unoccupied. What a relief! No waitresses suddenly crossing my path, no complex interplay of flashing lights and noise. Nothing to mess up what my doc calls "the Parkinsonian brain."

But the section wasn't empty. At the last table before the men's room, I passed a lady sitting quietly by herself, reading, drinking coffee. She glanced up, saw the walking stick, studied my face briefly, and said, "Sometimes my toes really bother me and it's hard to walk."

I nodded but said nothing, too busy concentrating on the next challenge, the bathroom door. The Parkinsonian brain has trouble with doorways, barriers, transitions. Revolving doors—kiss of death. The experts don't know why—something goes haywire as the brain processes sensory input. The legs sort of explode beneath me, like a blast of electricity has turned them into slow-motion jackhammers; meanwhile, the rest of me keeps right on going, and suddenly my whole body is pitching forward like it's marching down a steep hill.

Fortunately I managed the bathroom door without incident, and took care of necessities. Tapping my way back, I passed the nice lady again. She had been kind enough to start a conversation, so to be polite I said, "I guess you don't appreciate what you have until you lose it." She turned toward me, closed her book. "I had cancer, and it was a close call." I nodded, glanced at my feet. "Parkinson's."

She smiled, a grim smile, friendly, but hard-edged. The smile of a wounded soldier who'd briefly found a comrade-in-arms, someone who would hear what she had to say, so she would not be wasting her words.

"You have friends," she said. "You have people who care about you, who love you. But you have to face it alone."

I nodded. So true, I thought, as I inched forward, walking stick thwapping on the hardwood floor. So true. Each of us a solitary soul, trying to find our way, seeking guidance, friendship. But no one can do the seeking for us. Sometimes people think they can, but the ones who shout the loudest are the most afraid to face what the restaurant lady had faced: the betrayal of her body, the uncertainty, and the essential aloneness of every conscious soul. But from that solitude, we reach out, discover that there are others like us. We connect. We form communities—like the restaurant lady and me, solitary comrades.

My solitude meets yours. Somewhere there, in the middle, in the air between us, a door opens and a breath, a zephyr of love flows through. Invisible, fleeting, but is there anything more real? Anything more, somehow, permanent?

I greeted her smile with mine, tipped my head in her direction as she lowered her gaze and opened her book again. I turned back toward my friend. *Thwip, thwap, thwip-thwap.* Alone. Yes. But never alone. Yes. *Thwap, thwip.* Always . . . never . . . alone.

Of Dopamine I Sing

God Bless You Please, Mr. Parkinson

Last night I woke up singing,
And I couldn't remember why.
Then it hit me—I'd been dreaming
About a song I loved to sing.
But my body was unfamiliar,
It belonged to someone else.
I sat down at the piano
To play my melody,
But I could barely move my fingers
And the song got stuck inside me.
All I could do was say the words
And the words went something like this:

"Each day I got,
Is the best day I have,
It's the best darned day I got,
To get done what I got to do,
Because I got to, got to do it
No matter what comes my way,
Oh yes I do, yes I do . . . oh brother, yes I doooooo.

"I got to tell you—
Each day that I'm here,
Every mornin' noon and night,
It's the very very best day
That I'm ever gonna get,
So I'll take what that day gives me,

And give back all I got,
Because baby I'm gonna git there
To where I got to got to go,
I'm gonna give what I got to give,
'Til there's no more days to live
Ain't that the truth.

"And I'll get there,
Yes I'll get there,
Oh I will get there
Yes I AM gonna get there . . .

"Get there to where I got to got to gooooooooo."

Last night I woke up dreaming
That I'd forgotten where I lived.
I knew that I was someone,
But I couldn't remember who,
I had a lovely song to sing—
Lips moved—breath blew—
But I couldn't find the words.
Where did they go?
They must be here—somewhere—
A few—one or two
No more . . . no . . . more. . . .

Then I woke up and
I was me again
And that's
The end of
This
Silly
Song.

Festinatin' Rhythm

Every hour, I feel, is more
about every hour there's
more that I feel, more
about every day, I think,
is more and more
about each hour
I feel is me
and I think,
I am more
I am I
think
more
am I
I am
MIAMI!
AMINO!
I am
am I
ANEMONE,
MONOMANIA!!!
more
more
more
more
STOP
more
STOP
moremoremore
STOP!!!!!

Every hour, I feel,
is about each day
I am, I think, I
Am.

["fes-ti-na-tion (noun): involuntary, tottering walk characteristic of people with Parkinson's disease."
Word dictionary, online]

I Sing the Body #2, 2006

Conversation: There Is Always a Way
An E-mail Exchange With Jan Lipes

June 4, 2007. A date which will live in infamy. My Pearl Harbor. The beginning of the end, and the end of the beginning.

Yes, I know, I'm mixing Roosevelt and Churchill quotes, but the war metaphor fits: an unexpected life-and-death situation, a fight for survival against a superior enemy. Many people, most people have a day like that sometime in their lives. A day when their body fails, innocence is shattered, and harsh reality awaits. Turns out that often reality's not so bad, and it's where we should have been all along. But to get there, most of us need time, plus a little help from our friends.

Roughly six weeks after that fateful day when I learned about Trouble in Synapse City, I found myself on the phone with a guy named Jan Lipes. I'd never met the man but had heard a bit about his story—a painter, formerly a doctor, well known in the community, who was nearly quadriplegic due to advanced multiple sclerosis but still very active, wrote a column on art for a local newspaper, etc. He had called me in search of background about museum collection procedures and policies for a piece he was writing. As the conversation wound down, on a whim I said, "So Jan, we have something in common. We're brothers in progressive neurological disorders." I told him briefly about my recent Parkinson's diagnosis. His manner changed, and he was quiet when I finished. "I want to talk to you," he said.

A few days later, he was sitting across from me at the museum's café, listening and sharing stories, like a big brother starting to gently show his kid brother how to navigate the world. I was the newbie, Jan was the veteran, and I had a lot to learn. But we quickly realized that we had more in common than illness.

No friendship is common, but this one, given our backgrounds and proclivities, was unusual. We discovered intense and rewarding areas of shared experience, leading us to similar conclusions: the importance of empathy and its moral foundation; the balance between toleration and activism, acceptance and struggle; the joy of creativity; and above all a love of life and the need to persevere despite its many disappointments and inevitable losses.

Imagine our surprise when it became clear that we had arrived at this communion of thought from opposing directions—mine, while unorthodox, essentially religious. Jan's from a thorough grounding in existentialism and a complete rejection of religion. Instead of hurling slogans and weaponizing various forms of scripture from fortified castles, we enjoyed long afternoons of conversation in Jan's glass-enclosed den, watching the afternoon light dim into evening, letting the conversation flow.

When I stopped driving, we continued our friendship through the computer. We had to adjust. When Jan's right hand stopped working, he taught himself to paint with the other one. That's the thread woven through this e-mail exchange from the first few months of our friendship: there is always a way to squeeze a little more from the toothpaste tube of life. There is always a way. Until there isn't. That day will come. But not today.

I am grateful to Jan for his permission to print this exchange in a context that is foreign to his way of seeing things. Jan has taught me that existentialism can be an enlightened and tolerant way of life. He feels deeply that the only honest and grown-up view of reality is that the universe is empty and void, that this is the essential condition of life. With no higher power to lean on, we're each required to take responsibility ourselves for our decisions and their consequences. As he puts it:

"We all exist in the tiny sliver of light between infinite blackness before birth and after death. The logically inescapable conclusion is that all human activity is pointless. And especially pointless is artistic creation. Why bring something to life, why create 'a work of art' (not even on Darwin's bucket list for the propagation of the species) when death and nothingness will follow in short order?

"The answer to this philosophical conundrum entails a much overused and abused word, 'nobility.' If there is anything 'noble' about human beings, anything at all, it is the capacity to recognize that death is the end of all our efforts and that despite this stark fact (or perhaps, because of it), we choose to continue to work, to live, to love. WE ARE AWARE AND WE CHOOSE."

To Jan's way of thinking, if we pick up the phone and punch in 1-800-DIAL-GOD, and all we ever hear is "This line is out of service," then suddenly we're faced with a terrifying prospect: freedom. Complete freedom. No one to tell us what to do, no one to blame, just you and me trying to work, live, and love. How do we do that without hurting each other? Can we make the necessary leap of imagination and try to walk in our neighbor's shoes? Can we learn to work together to make our lives better? Those questions sound like winners to me, whatever path one takes to get there. Many people, religious and otherwise, who profess similar values could learn much from my caring and courageous friend.

Jan Lipes, September 3, 2013

BHP, January 14, 2012
Photo: Jan Lipes

Aug 3, 2007, 7:29 PM

Brian,

Thank you for your message—I, too, greatly enjoyed our conversation at the museum. On the subject of illness, I believe a cataclysmic natural phenomenon such as a thunderstorm or avalanche is part of the same "nature" that causes us to have pneumonia or a stroke. Nature is nature, within and without.

You spoke of the concept of embracing the disease. In the Bhagavad Gita, it's said, "One to me is shame or fame, one to me is pain or gain." I'd like to talk about this with you sometime. Also the two sides of self-knowledge. The knowledge of the intellect and the knowledge of the body.

Brian, I empathize with you, and I use that word in its most profound sense. You and I are fellow travelers, and we have art to sustain us.

Best regards,
Jan

Aug 4, 2007, 10:54 PM

Hi Jan—

I like the "nature" idea—the molecules that make up my body and your body are essentially the same as the molecules that make up the thunderstorm and the avalanche. I know, the specific molecular structure is different, but they're all vibrating at the same frequency as it were. Connected. There's no such thing as "man vs. nature" or even "man and nature"—there is just nature. Even disease and death—nature. I tend to see disease as a cataclysmic exterior event—an invasion of something foreign—when in fact, in some strange way, it's still me.

I can't remember what I said about embracing the disease—frankly, that sounds too good to be true. Something "Saint Brian" would say, not the terrified lump of flesh that I really am. Pain and gain are not one to me, though I suppose that's something to be desired. But maybe that cosmic detachment is not the only direction to go.

The only way to deal with this thing emotionally is not to go around it, but go through it. In other words, trust my feelings on a given day—if I am feeling grief, then feel it—same with anger, fear, etc. I don't need to act all this out. I just need to open the door to it, invite it into my room so to speak, let it have its way with me, but internally. I see this as a way of keeping me grounded, in touch with my internal reality. It's an act of trust, that basically says, Brian, your body may be sick, but YOU are not sick. What you're feeling is what you need to feel. It's okay.

Sometime we will have to talk more about that "knowledge of the body" thing. I suspect there's some good conversation there.

Keep in touch!
Brian

Aug 8, 2007, 12:58 PM

Brian

Yes, I certainly agree. It's the same nature, within and without. We have "free will," but that means very little . . . nature is going to trump you every time.

And I'm no saint either, though I do think nonattachment is something to take seriously. Sometimes when I'm in pain, I'm able to relax and let the words flow through my brain and I feel less discomfort. But most of the time, it's just plain tough to get through.

Your approach—going with your feelings—is absolutely the best. You are giving yourself permission to feel your present . . . I can't think of anything healthier.

Knowledge "with the body" takes time. We all discover what it means eventually.

I hope you are well today. Do you have a problem with the heat?

Jan

Aug 13, 2007, 11:36 AM

Hi Jan—

Last questions first. I'm grateful that you ask! I feel that I am so in the early stages of this thing, compared to veterans like you, that my issues barely register on the Complaint-O-Meter. Physical—won't bore you with the blow-by-blow, but the invisible enemy advances on many fronts. The inexorability of the thing is what's so disturbing, and the individual variability. But whatever patterns it starts out with continue. If it moves faster in the early stages, it will continue to move faster, and the long-term prognosis gets worse. My doc says she sees nothing particularly unusual going on, but that doesn't keep me from worrying. I'm weathering the drug pretty well—the first week was tough. But it settled down.

Emotionally—the usual ups and downs. I would say, as long as I'm working, I'm happy. Last night, as I looked at one of the new prints, I felt that deep sense of satisfaction—I would even say, joy—that I've always felt when the work has gone well.

By the way, I'm fascinated with all that nonattachment stuff, especially the Japanese variety. Somehow the Zen masters are fully alive, immersed in each moment, but also calm, unattached—able to see far and feel deeply, but on the surface, smooth as glass. I admire them and want to learn what I can from them. It's just not where I live. I have to deal with what life throws at me in my own way. If I'm not doing my emotional homework, that sense of inner balance goes away, and I have to work hard to get it back. That's about as close as I come to the Zen stuff. I really don't want to be unattached—I want to be completely attached, to my emotional life, to life itself.

I'm just doing what I need to do every day to keep my ship afloat.

Thanks again for your friendship and concern!

Brian

Aug 13, 2007, 7:29 PM

Brian:

I remember waking up one beautiful summer Saturday way back in 1981 . . . putting on a white golf shirt, green shorts, and white sneakers, and going out for a run. I ran about two miles. As I was doing the last 500 feet to my house, I began to feel the most peculiar thing. It was as if something began to hold my legs back, to make them hard to lift, as if an invisible band had been tied around them. When I got home, I mentioned it to my wife, then forgot about it. That was that, and I went about my business. But I VIVIDLY remember the sensation of having my motion impeded . . . it was so strange and so disturbing. Later came the storm.

The most peculiar sensations arise with central nervous system disease . . . it's just something completely outside our experience, until it happens.

As you described noticing things that others don't, I was flooded with all sorts of feelings. It is absolutely phenomenal to discover that no one can ever REALLY know what you are feeling. Wives come very close, but even they can't fully know. This is one of those things where stuff you knew intellectually, say in your twenties, is never REALLY comprehended until you go through something like this. Which relates to the issue of empathy; what it means, who you get it from, and what its limits are.

Gosh, Brian, there is simply too much to say and as usual my mind is all over the place, seeking, searching, mixing it up, deconstructing, and reassembling. Please forgive the untidiness of my mind.

You know I am typing with my non-dominant hand, my left (I'll give you my left if you give me your right; I could write a book in one night!).

When I'm painting, my mind is FULLY engaged. I'm aware of nothing but the linen and paint. All pain is gone. All of the myriad of symptoms MS devilishly tosses at me vanish. It is magic. The very second I put my brush down, I feel like crap. I've always been a workaholic, but now it's even worse. It's almost as if I'm going to commit workaholicide. The one thing I fear most is losing the ability to work. Of course, we are marvelously adaptive creatures. When I couldn't do emergency medicine anymore, I became an administrator. When I didn't want to do that anymore, I reverted to my grand passion . . . art. I couldn't use my dominant right hand, so I began painting with my left. I drive a three-ton vehicle down to Philly with one hand. THERE IS ALWAYS A WAY.

You've got to do whatever works for you. Art is what connects me with life. I see absolutely everything through the prism of art. It is how I remain engaged with this world.

To be continued . . .

Warmest regards

Jan

Aug 14, 2007, 10:41 AM

There is always a way. I need to hear that.

I had an epiphany last night: With all the work I do to stay centered, stay balanced, weather the emotional storms, etc.—it suddenly hit me: Brian, you have to fight for what you want. Cowboy up, as they say. At that moment I felt capable of doing whatever needs to be done. We'll see how I do down the road. I can only fight today's battles.

I want to compliment you on your column about death camp art. A guy who collects art made in horrifying prisons—an interesting choice for your column, written by a man who is, himself, in a kind of prison, a physical prison that presents him with unimaginable obstacles to his creativity—a man who also, in his own way, writes waltzes on a piece of toilet paper, tangos on a scrap of cloth.

There is always a way.

Maybe the most essential ingredient of life is—just being alive, and our desire to live it out, all the way. I've been haunted by something my sister said to me in her final months, after all the chemo and surgeries, and it was finally becoming clear that she had nothing left to try, no hope. Something very simple: "I want to live!" But the way she said it! I will always remember.

I'm off to Montana on Thursday for a week, to see my aging parents. That's another ongoing drama . . .

Brian

Aug 16, 2007, 9:28 PM

Brian

Re what you said about prison, I wrote a column some years ago about a convicted murderer named Ronny Wilson. He is in prison and he paints using dye from M&Ms that he melts down and applies to his "canvases" with a "paintbrush" made from toothpicks and his own hair. I was intrigued and wrote a column about the guy using his real name. It began something like this: "We are murderers, we are rapists, we are thieves . . . we are artists." Guaranteed to catch the eye of your typical Bucks County matron, right?

Well, it also caught the eye of a good friend of the murderer. He wrote me an e-mail from New Mexico where this guy is in prison. It went something like this: "I am a good friend of Ronny Wilson and I am not sure that he would be pleased at the way you characterized him in your column. In fact, I AM SURE HE WOULD NOT BE PLEASED." "Holy crap," I thought. "I'm up the creek as a newbie to the journalism game." Not only did I not write "any resemblance to persons living or dead, blah blah blah," but I went out of my way to use the real guy's name! STUPID!

I had visions of getting slammed by some hoodlum friend of his on my way to the grocery store one day . . .

Well, I thought about it and finally wrote back to him: "Do you think I write these columns to get rich, for the $1.98 I make per column, for profit? For fame? For FUN? I'll tell you EXACTLY why I write these columns and why I wrote about Wilson. BECAUSE I TOO AM

IN PRISON, IN A WHEELCHAIR. BECAUSE I KNOW WHAT IT MEANS TO OVERCOME OBSTACLES. BECAUSE I KNOW WHAT IT'S LIKE TO MAKE ART OUT OF A JAIL CELL SO IMPLACABLE THAT I CAN IDENTIFY WITH MR. WILSON AND ADMIRE HIS STRUGGLE TO CREATE IN THE MOST IMPOSSIBLE OF CIRCUMSTANCES."

That was the truth.

I got a reply saying, "Now I understand. Peace." One of my more thrilling moments (which no one knows about except you) as a journalist!

There is always a way.

I am deeply sorry about your sister.

Warmest wishes
Jan

Aug 25, 2007, 12:21 AM

Jan—

Just back from Montana—was there for a week or so with my brother and my parents. Travel— how different it feels now, less than three months into this adventure. I was struck by how unforgiving the world is. Call it a very tiny introduction to what you described, sitting in your wheelchair by the entrance of the Michener waiting for someone to open the door. My plane out of Philly was delayed—missed my connection—had to spend the night in Denver and get up early the next morning. Wore me out, I guess. Sitting in my seat on the runway, I started to feel lightheaded, nauseated—suddenly couldn't see too well, and nearly passed out. Clearly a drug side effect, never experienced before, but described in the patient info. Unable to lie down, unable to go to the bathroom because we were in the process of taking off. Looked frantically for the barf bag— fortunately didn't need it, but it was touch and go for a while. Unforgiving.

Coming back, an evening flight, due in to Philly at 10:30. Plane was delayed for over an hour and a half, didn't get in until 12:15. Waited for a half hour for the parking shuttle. Didn't get home until 2 AM. Unforgiving.

Standing there at Zone 3, Terminal D, smelling the exhaust from all the buses, watching shuttle after shuttle go by, feeling those strange internal tremors that come at the end of the drug cycle, it hit me—this world is just not made for someone with Parkinson's disease. Quite a revelation, eh? As you say, this is how we learn about where empathy comes from, and learn about its limits.

So let's talk about that. As an intelligent and basically caring person, I already knew that weighty truth about the world and disease. But now—I KNOW it. Facing eventual disability myself, there's an intensity to what I feel. And I extend that feeling outward in ways that are new to me. Toward you, for instance. I relay my little travel drama, knowing that you will connect with it, but all the while saying to myself—"Jan would love to have your problems!" Your little aside—"I'll give you my left hand if you give me your right"—now that's honesty, my friend.

A hard question—okay—would I do it? Honest answer—I might loan it to you for a while. Or I might trade left hands with you, since mine still works a lot better than yours—though it ain't what it used to be. But I NEED that right hand. It's the best thing I have—it's still almost normal, though the strange shakiness when I move it (cogwheel rigidity) is often there, and each time I see it, I'm terrified. How long before the right hand is as stiff as the left hand is now? How long before they're both in bad shape? And I'm facing that functionality problem we've been discussing, almost as intensely as you are: THERE'S ALWAYS A WAY. But for how long? No one can tell me.

So where is my newfound wondrous empathy? It's there. I feel your situation—your prison—in a way that was unknown to me before. But push comes to shove, I won't trade my right hand for your left. Sorry. Does this mean that separateness wins out in the end? No. But I guess it does mean that there's an ongoing, fluid balance between empathy and separateness. Total empathy would mean there is no self left for anyone to connect with. Total separateness—that would be the worst kind of prison imaginable (even worse than yours, I think)—a complete lack of empathic connection—the mind of the sociopath, and the source of much evil in this world.

So—enough of that. I thank you for your prison story. For now, as the friend of your murderer said, I understand, as best I can. Peace.

Brian

Aug 26, 2007, 7:41 PM

Brian

Glad you are back. I hope your parents and brother are well.

Travel is difficult. "Unforgiving" is exactly right. I have many, many travel stories such as you described . . . some relatively benign, some disastrous. Over time these delightful anecdotes may find their way into our conversation (lucky you!), but suffice it to say that in my situation, I simply don't travel anymore. The world is not, as you say, made for the ill. It doesn't even take us into account! It's very sad for this guy here, who has a heart for France like Tony Bennett does for Frisco.

I was talking to a friend I've known for forty years the other day. At one point, I griped that I would never walk in the surf by the ocean again. NEVER. His response was, "Yeah, well, you know they have those wheelchairs that go right into the surf."

Think about it. Walking in the surf at 5 AM is one of the greatest "freedoms" we can have in this life. The sound of the ocean, the light, the sea smells, the crashing of the waves. What drama! What joy!

Yes, I could have someone wheel me down to the surf in one of those goofy contraptions. Then I could sit still and stare. Then I could wait for someone to wheel me back.

It CAN be done, but the very nature of the experience becomes the antithesis of what it's supposed to be. Instead of the joy of independence, I have to confront my hopeless dependence. Instead of freedom of movement, I have to confront the prison of immobility. Instead of the drama before me, I am swallowed up by the angst within my breast.

It is tough. And I have to be tough. There are so many instances where this principle of diminished "quality of life" comes into play that I can't even begin to enumerate them. My life is replete with them, morning, noon, and night. I have to be very mentally tough to accept life on these terms.

It's okay that you don't want to trade hands. I understand completely. Often, when I see a guy walking down the street, I say to myself, why can't I have HIS nervous system? I'd like a transplant. But there's a slight problem. It's taken fifty-five years of hard work to build me. If I took his nervous system, I could dance and run and hump like a monkey, but I wouldn't be ME anymore.

Most times I prefer to remain me. There are times, however, when I want to get the hell out of this carcass of a prison no matter what the cost.

Empathy should be spelled with a capital E.

Listen, my friend. I don't know if I should be talking to you like this. I don't want to bring you down, especially when you have every reason to hope for many years of freedom. I am just relating my experiences, as you are relating yours. There is some commonality . . . but vast differences as well, of course.

I should probably just write when I am a happy camper.

Best regards

Jan

Aug 30, 2007, 11:54 PM

Jan—

You know, I'm very grateful for this latest e-mail you sent. It's intensely honest, and I'm glad you don't feel you have to pull any punches with me. I read your words about what you no longer have in your life, and will never have again, and my empathy fails me. I can't remotely pretend that I know what it's like to be you, but I'm willing to listen and learn. As painful and difficult as my life has become since the diagnosis, I look at your life, and what you've had to deal with, and, well, there's really no comparison. I had almost fifty-four years of healthy existence, and I used it well. That is a great comfort to me as I face my diminished future. You've had to deal with this stuff since your late twenties, and have had to overcome tremendous hardship to do the kind of things that, until now, I've simply taken for granted.

Given these brutal differences in our experience, I can't tell you what it's meant to me that you've been so generous—that you've listened so attentively to what I've been feeling. You have shown me empathy, with that capital E, in a way that only someone who lives in your prison can.

The last couple days I've been in a dark place inside. I just can't believe this is happening to me. I love my life, I love my body, and now both are being taken from me. I'm not ready for this. Just not ready. What choice do I have but to live this thing out? To find, as you say, that inner toughness. I'm working on that.

Hope for the best, but plan for the worst—that's been my mantra. I hope I have many years of freedom, but I'm living as if I don't. Thankfully I have my photographs—this body of work I've been doing. Sometimes I just get on a roll and pour my feelings into these pictures, and often they're not pretty.

So that's some of what's going on in the life of Brian—thanks for letting me vent a bit. And thanks again for trusting me enough to vent, yourself.

All for now—
Brian

Sep 2, 2007, 5:39 PM

Brian

I won't bullshit you. If you want to talk, we'll talk. I'm not interested in polite garbage, which belongs at cocktail parties. I'll tell you what I see as I see it. I expect the same from you. I understand only too well the limits of human empathy. I'm not surprised when I bump up against these limits, though sometimes it infuriates me. The human condition dictates that empathy has limits. There are highly unusual exceptions, of course; I think of Mother Teresa, Gandhi, and some others in that regard. But perhaps they weren't human but rather divine.

I'm very grateful you are willing to listen. As far as comparisons go, I don't really want to go there. When I practiced medicine, I never made judgments about people in terms of the severity of their illness. I still don't. Everybody deals with their own problems to the best of their abilities. One man's broken femur is another man's hangnail. What some people find is easy to cope with, other people find impossible. We have to respect everyone's situation and ability to cope. Yes, we have differences, but we also have similarities . . . let's continue to explore those as long as it's productive to do so.

"I love my life," you said. That is a powerful, fabulous thing to say. Those of us who do, and who are aware that we do, are very fortunate. "Anyone who loves their life will know how to defend it," Henry James once said. I believe this is true. It is related to the idea that there is always a way.

To "hope for the best and plan for the worst" also strikes a very familiar chord. When I realized my diagnosis (and I'M the one who made it), the very first question I asked myself in a dispassionate, coldly rational way was, "How will you support your family as a quadriplegic?" That was the worst that could happen, far worse than dying. Well, today, I'm three-quarters of the way there, the kids are grown up and self-supporting, and I'm still working . . . a quarter century later! There is always a way.

"Living as if you don't have many years of freedom" is the best way to live, the only way to live. The life force is very, very strong . . . I remember Alfred Hitchcock, in discussing a murder in one of his films, saying that it's a very, very hard thing to kill someone. He meant that the victim doesn't die very easily. But at the same time, life is so fragile. If you're depressed one day, which impairs your immune system, and a little clump of cancer cells (which starts growing in our bodies every day) doesn't get zapped the way it normally does, bam! You're out of the picture.

Well, my friend, enough for now.

Best regards

Jan

Sep 5, 2007, 10:55 PM

Hi Jan—

You're wise not to compare different situations—makes me think that you must have been a great doctor. Yes—respect everyone's situation and cope—true. But then again, it's productive to explore BOTH differences and similarities. I want to hear about what your average day is really like, and that means, often, differences. Much of my angst with my recent diagnosis has more to do with the future—with greatly diminished possibilities time-wise, and a great sense of loss from that—rather than severe physical problems. I'm terrified of the major league bodily destruction, but haven't experienced it—yet. You have. That's a difference that's worth exploring. So don't hold back.

For me, lately, I've been fretting about certain reactions I continue to get from important people in my life, who seem determined to distance themselves—kind of like your friend who told you to get a different wheelchair so you could wheel it on the beach. Amazing. I often hear about the people with PD who go for decades with almost no problems. As if that's supposed to make me feel better! I've explained to these folks the true nature of this disease, based on the thorough research I've done. It would be monumentally stupid for me to blithely assume that I will sail through problem-free for the next twenty years! People tell themselves that it will make me feel better to hear those optimistic stories, but it makes me burn inside.

You know Bri, you have a dread disease, but don't worry, be happy, because Mr. X or Ms. Y did fine. Or—Bri, those wonderful scientists are going to fix things with some new miracle drug. But I've explained—they don't really have much of a clue what causes the disease! Even the high-powered expert who wrote the encyclopedic book I've been reading says that if they don't know what causes it, there's not much hope of curing it. People have been saying this stuff to Parkinson's patients for decades, and frankly, I think it's cruel and I don't buy it. I have to deal with reality, and the reality is, there is a likelihood that in my lifetime they will get increasingly better at treating symptoms but not at dealing with the underlying condition. There is NOTHING out there now that slows the thing down one iota. Nothing. That is reality. Mr. P will have his way with me. The drugs will make the journey more tolerable, and I'm thankful for that. But I have to deal with the certainty of eventual destruction, and the uncertainty of the timing.

The larger point is that I'm learning that illness is both an opportunity for, and a barrier to, empathy—depending on the people involved.

Now I'm going to make a few scans. *Bonne nuit*!

Brian

Sep 10, 2007, 9:01 AM

Hi Brian

Our approach regarding the truth about the disease process is quite similar. I've met the sorts of people you mention, and armies more. I've always maintained that without knowing the cause of the disease, no rational cure could be developed. Having seen my mother recently go into complete remission after treatment for a very large lymphoma, I can't really say that anymore. I will say this . . . with the human genome mapped, anything is possible. The problem for diseases such as MS and Parkinson's is that with our capitalist ethos, the market share is too small. R&D costs too much for the big guys to aggressively pursue study of less pervasive neurologic disorders.

One of the more tragic events I watched repeatedly during my career in medicine was the hope of certain patients, especially those with cancer, being raised, dashed, raised, dashed . . . over and over again. It was really heartbreaking. Like you, I resolved never to be suckered in by phony hopes. I therefore gritted my teeth and hoped for the best but accepted the worst.

I don't believe you are wallowing but rather in a period of coming to terms with this disorder. This takes time . . . much time. Your work is proof positive of your ongoing love of, and engagement with, life.

Best regards for now,
Jan

Sep 15, 2007, 12:31 AM

Hi Jan—

Interesting what you say about the drug companies and research. Hadn't thought of that. Also interesting what you say about your mother's remission and its implications for our attitudes about curing our respective maladies. Maybe there is a shred of hope, though I must say—and I might not confess this to anyone but you—I am increasingly fatalistic about my situation. There are no remissions with Parkinson's—just a long day's journey into night, to quote the playwright. Yes, that journey is made easier with the drugs, surgeries, etc., but nothing can stop it. Nothing. There are a few drugs for which "neuroprotective" claims have been made, but these are highly controversial, and the best experts I've come across are careful to distance themselves from those claims.

On the "reality of my days" front—today was one of those dark days. I saw the neurologist again yesterday and decided to pin her down on the prognosis front. So far she has taken the "individualized" and "unpredictable" direction, and she is right to do so. On the other hand, I've gradually learned that there is a sort of bell curve to this entity. I can reasonably expect a few years of decent functionality—three, four, five perhaps—but by the time people are into this thing maybe seven, eight, ten years, they are experiencing significant, debilitating problems. And it's downhill from there. I asked the doctor point-blank if this is the most likely scenario, and she said, "Yes."

Then there are those "wonder drugs" that everyone talks about, as if they are a panacea. They ain't. For eight weeks now I've been engaged in a little experiment with my body, raising the dose of the dopamine agonist I'm taking. Finally I've climbed the mountain, reached the nirvana of nine milligrams per day, a significantly therapeutic dose. Has it helped? Yes. But only in that the symptoms are reduced, and intermittently at that. This is the reality of the drugs—they make your life more tolerable, but they are imperfect and marginally effective, and their effectiveness is directly related to the amount of side effects that you can put up with.

Jan, my life is beautiful—I work, and I am surrounded by love and fulfillment—my days are incredibly happy. In religious terms, I am given each day my daily bread. But each day has also become an agony, a terror. I don't know how to live in these circumstances. I want to hang on to my days, squeeze them into a box, never let them go. Because every day that passes is one day closer to the brutal destruction of my lovely home, this thing that I am. I understand that this is the nature of our lives—but that's another one of those well-meaning platitudes that distract me from the reality of what I'm facing. It's different now. The very routine of life—the way the days pass, the weeks pass, the seasons pass—has become painful to me. And I feel the presence of death in my body as I never have before. Not as an abstraction, a construct—a reality.

I take a break at lunchtime on workdays and drive my car into a little wooded place near our staff parking lot. I look up into the leaves, the sky, and try to get in touch with whatever feelings I had to repress in order to accomplish all the administrative tasks of the morning. Today I felt grief. Nothing but a silent, wordless grief. I just didn't think my life would unfold this way.

Beautiful and terrible. The agony and the ecstasy. Too bad that phrase was ruined by Charlton Heston trying to be Michelangelo! Because that's what life is. Man, am I learning that lesson! Well, I may not prevail, but I will persevere and do the work I've been given to do. I'm one of those musicians on the deck of the *Titanic*, and I will play my song for all it's worth.

All for now—
Brian

Sep 19, 2007, 3:23 PM

Hi Brian

Isn't all of life a long slow journey into night? Isn't this thing we call life, to paraphrase someone, a thin sliver of light between two vast, dark eternities?

Prognostics are notoriously unreliable. Again, don't misunderstand me. It's just that I am skeptical about EVERYTHING, both good and bad. Death resides within all our breasts from the moment we are born and certainly after the age of seventeen. We humans simply deny the reality of mortality until we are forced to confront it. I have always been sensitive to the passage of time, and it has often been associated with remorse. This is one of the reasons that I believe the camera is the most potent weapon on earth; it's the only tool that can STOP time. This is why I have been so anal about being the keeper of all the old family photos, which I have begun delving into in order to discover some mystery, I'm not quite sure what.

You are in such an early part of this voyage. You are still grieving.

Brian, let's think about another get-together soon. I think we need facial expressions, body language, the voice and bodily presence every once in a while to augment these written discussions.

If you think that's a good idea, send me the times that are usually best for you.

warmest.

Jan

Sep 23, 2007, 10:04 PM

Hmmm—are you thinking of that rather amazing line in *Waiting for Godot*? Goes something like this: "A woman giving birth straddles the grave—a brief flash of light, then darkness."

Actually I don't see life that way at all, believe it or not—despite my moody ministrations of late. I've always thought that the existential nihilism of Beckett and crew was a dead end. Or to be more honest—it just doesn't correspond to my experience of life. I'm more of an Emersonian kind of guy—maybe a Wordsworthian—you know, those "intimations." I've had my own "intimations" over the years, enough to convince me absolutely that there is more to this thing we're part of— this reality thing—than meets the eye. Ask me my favorite American painter of the nineteenth century, and I will reply without hesitation—George Inness—a transcendentalist who saw magic and light in the world, everywhere, at least in his later work. That should tell you something about where my head is at.

None of which changes the visceral way I respond to my situation, and you're right—I'm just starting down this road, and there's a lot of grieving to do. And a lot of anger to work through my system. This is one reason why I've been grateful for our correspondence—the perspective of the veteran is something I can really use. Please, as I've said, always feel free to let fly with whatever you feel moved to share with me.

I think it would be nice to work out some, as they say, face time. Let me check my calendar up at work and see what things look like.

Brian

Sep 25, 2007, 2:52 PM

Brian

No, it wasn't Beckett's line. Someone else whom I paraphrased fairly accurately. Can't remember who . . .

I've been an existentialist (E) since my college years. NOT a nihilist, however. Do you see the two as connected? Many people think of E as nihilistic, atheistic, and negative about life. I have never seen this philosophy in that way. The term E is used very loosely and, I find, often with little understanding. It is used frequently as a kind of fuzzy synonym for the intellectually morose, grim, self-preoccupied, and pessimistic.

When I discovered E through my readings in college . . . my first and perhaps deepest impression was by Camus's "The Myth of Sisyphus" . . . I was astounded. It was an epiphany for me. I went on to read as much E as I could, starting with Pascal. (I never saw Beckett as contributing in any substantial way to this philosophy.)

For me, E is an optimistic philosophy, and one that, instead of demeaning man with the "humiliated thought" of traditional religions, ennobles him. E stresses the centrality of free will in human life. E means looking into the void, which I believe is the underlying "reality" of existence, confronting it, and having the courage to go on IN SPITE OF IT. It is, ultimately, a philosophy of rebellion against the constraints of the human condition. It is the desire to live and create despite seeing, with open eyes, the nothingness underlying life. E requires great strength of character.

Some have other frameworks upon which to build: other beliefs, other value systems, other priorities. I have embraced E because it exalts man's reason, acknowledges responsibility for one's actions, and confers dignity. I might also add, as an aside, this philosophy has provided me with tremendous coping abilities in dealing with MS.

Intimations . . . of mortality. when I first read this fellow, Wordsworth, I didn't have a clue. Then I was a mere babe with everything before me (running around the hilltops like Wordsworth himself, as a young man). I've had plenty of intimations of mortality since then. Enough with the intimations, already!

Inness was a wonderful painter. Good choice. I don't have a favorite nineteenth-century American painter.

In another vein, I am very angry too. This has been going on since 1983. I feel cheated. I've been robbed of precious moments in life too numerous to count, and the thievery goes on. But I've also been blessed (no divinity nonsense implied). Without the gigantic kick in the ass of MS, I might never have become an artist, the finest way of being that I have found in my life. So the anger is just part of the picture; the other side of the coin is the astounding new life in art I have found.

all the best,
jan

Sep 28, 2007, 11:50 PM

Hi Jan—

Hard to know where to begin with this one—such a big subject! I think we have to start our dialogue with a simple truth. Your experience and mine are very different. I place no value judgment on this. It's just that when people talk about this stuff, they often build up these huge logical structures to defend their positions, when the basic reality, the starting point, is that we experience life differently. I don't feel that void, that nothingness underlying life. You do. Why is that? I know someone who is a high-powered geneticist at Penn—his beloved wife (recently deceased from cancer) was deeply religious; he is not. He once told me, without bias or rancor, that he thought there must be a genetic predisposition for religion. He wasn't saying that to insult or somehow demean religion—he loved his wife dearly and respected her choices. He was just offering an explanation for why you experience a void as the underlying reality, and I don't.

Given that our experience is so different, how do we even talk about this without the conversation devolving into a petty squabble? Which, by the way, is so often the state of the discourse between the "opposing sides." I think we can start by honoring the differences but also exploring the similarities, especially in terms of shared values. I'm interested in your emphasis on the centrality of free will. I'm interested in the importance of rebellion. I'm interested in the desire to live and create—and in the need for strength of character. If we explore these things with open minds, I suspect we will find that our different paths sometimes lead to the same, or similar, places. At the very least we can wave to each other on the way, and maybe once in a while we can even sit around the campfire and toast a few marshmallows.

Brian

Oct 1, 2007, 9:38 PM

Brian

Your geneticist friend was, as one might expect, seeing the world through the eyes of . . . well, a geneticist. But I think he was right to an extent. Certainly, you can't go too far astray nowadays if you say that something is the result of the interaction of the genome AND the environment. Many things in life fall into this categorization. Does religion?

I have no ax to grind, and I hope I didn't give you the impression that I was preaching. I am what I am. I am the product of my genes and my life experience. The same applies to you. As the French so wisely say, "Vive la différence!" Catholics, Jews, Muslims, Atheists, Protestants, Buddhists, etc. etc. etc. . . . there's a place for everyone in this life. And no one owns the truth. I accept whatever another person's beliefs are and hope they can follow the same path.

We all have a lot more in common than not. These endpoints of coping with the trauma of life . . . disease, etc. . . . are critical. There is not only one way to come to terms with it all. Each of us has our own way.

Jan

Nov 18, 2007, 7:52 PM

Hi Jan—

Only a quick note for now—tomorrow a great horde of Petersons is descending upon us for the holiday, and Helen and I have been going crazy with preparations.

Friday—can't tell you how much that afternoon meant to me. I am so grateful for your generosity, sharing so much with me. A beautiful moment—as the light faded into twilight, sitting there in the darkening house, talking about life—choosing life—using up all the life we've been given—giving until there's nothing left to give. That moment has stayed with me, and will stay with me for a long time.

We shall have more of those moments, and in the meantime, we have the wonders of cyberspace. Keep sending me your thoughts, and I will do the same!

Your friend,
Brian

Jan Lipes, *Summer New Hope*, oil on linen, 30 x 40 inches

Jan Lipes, *The Artist's Mother*, 2008, oil on canvas, 30 x 30 inches

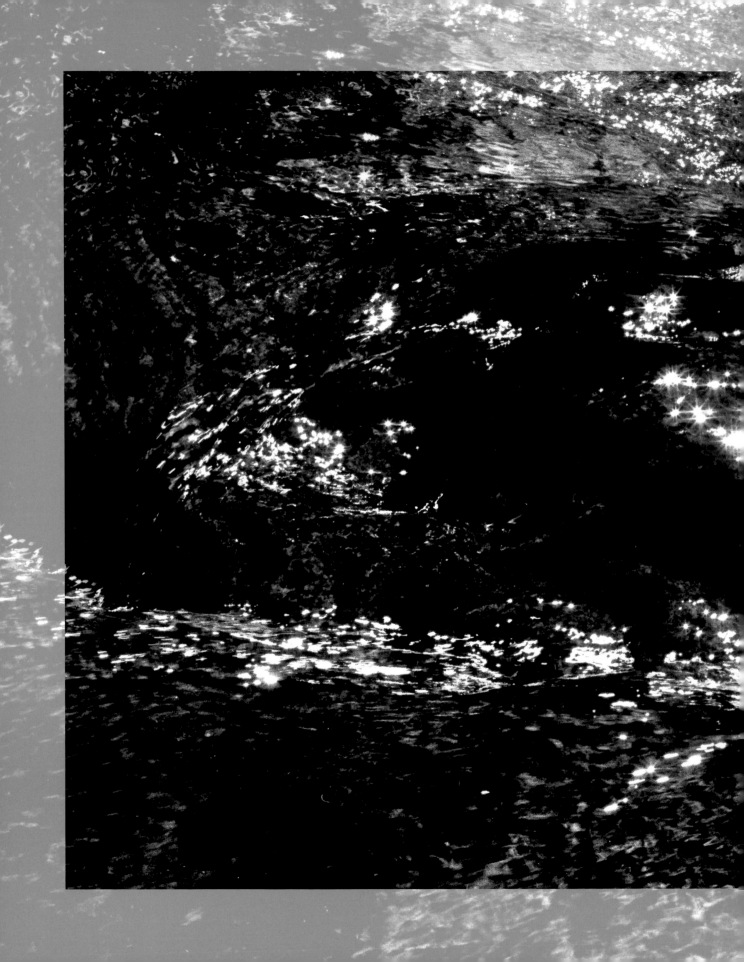

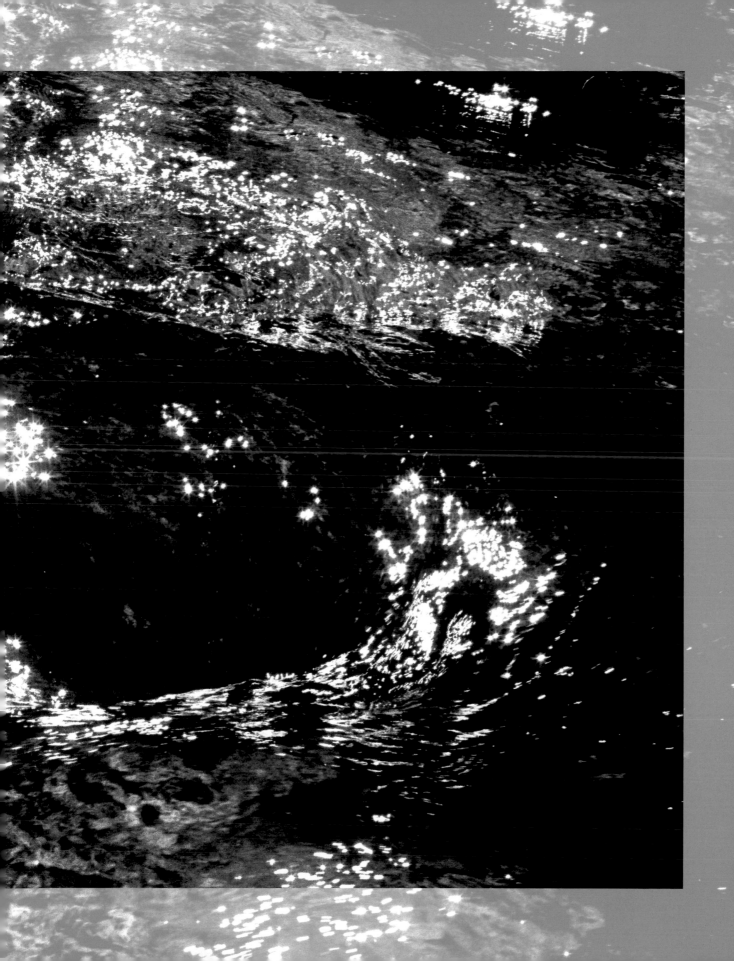

Why?

Every blade of grass, every dirt clod, every atom of every speck of dust and fleck of rust and every vein of molten rock in the earth's dark core, each and every molecular worldly thing, is bursting, exploding, pouring out, and gushing forth with meaning, purpose, poetry; with music and magic and wild creative madness. Everything is alive, aware. Everywhere.

Same blade of grass, same clod of dirt, same dust, rust, and molten rock. Okay, there they are. So what? The earth turns on its axis, the galaxy spins at a hundred million miles per nanosecond or however fast respectable galaxies go, and if anybody anywhere thinks grass and dirt and galaxies care about human beings and our collective fantasies, or were manufactured in a vast interstellar factory as part of some mysterious plan for ultimate harmony and well-being—I invite you to spend some time in this world as it is.

The earth brings forth its joyous creative cornucopia. Then an earthquake collapses an undersea mountain stirring up a wall of water that kills ten thousand children with their whole lives to live.

So, I want to know: Was the world made? Is it a created thing? Or did it just happen?

Many people insist, and are correct in saying, that a blade of grass is a collection of biological processes inhabiting a particular clump of molecules governed by a set of rules and axioms that control all blades of grass and dirt clods and galaxies. No more, no less, that's the way it was, is, and will be.

But how could something so perfect, yet so ordinary, be accidental?

Many people insist, correctly, that a blade of grass's perfection is an illusion that's real only because we've all decided it's real. But why does the beauty of that single blade of grass stir me down to my very roots and imprint itself on my soul, grab me like an errant puppy and shake me and wake me up and make me spend my life doing nothing but sing about it?

Let's say the universe *was* made, by someone, or something, through some unknowable combination of time, process and purpose.

Why is the world the way it is?

Why make a universe overflowing with meaning, that is also utterly meaningless? Why make a universe governed by random impersonal events, where everything that happens is also part of a mysterious tapestry of veiled intentionality?

Why is this moment, right now, a moment in which anything that's possible might happen, when new stars are born as galaxies collide, seeds burst out of the earth, thoughts appear that have never been thought before? All that and more, much more.

Why is this moment, right now, already gone, and I reach back to catch it but catch a handful of air, and I turn around to see what's coming and all I see are stars dying and galaxies flying off into empty space and the seed that grows and the thoughts that soar are falling down, down, as all that is crumbles into nothingness.

What is this place?

The bottomless abyss. The light that rises out of the earth like a fountain, filling the sky.

Pain and terror and utter abandonment. Purpose and love and creativity beyond imagining.

Why? Maybe there is no reason why. But think about it . . . think of other ways it could be . . . if where we are was not so fundamentally contradictory but predictable, consistent . . . think . . . uncertainty, confusion, mistakes, failure, loss, emptiness—take these away and what's left?

I want to know. What is the loam, the necessary substrate? What is the layer of nutrient at the bottom of the petri dish?

Is this a place that's forever making and remaking itself? I'm just asking. No—that's the wrong question. Is this a place where anything can happen, but nothing is actual until it can become something more than just a possibility? I need to understand.

Still, not the right question. All those painful contradictions—what if life was always full and never empty, all light and no abyss, only joy and no terror—what kind of place would we be calling our home? A place where everything that could happen has already happened? A place where there are no stories—because the whole point of a story is, what's going to happen? And you don't know the answer until you tell the story, live the story?

A story is a good story when there are choices to be made. The consequences are real and dangerous. People die. Sometimes we do bad things. We fail and dream of better places but never get there.

Is this broken, ambivalent world the only world that could be made where what we do matters? Where there are no answers to any of these questions except each one of us, each of our lives, is an answer to a question, and that question is, what's going to happen next and how will it all turn out?

If there really was a cosmic road map that always told us where to turn, then there would be no stories. And there would be no "us," the human race, post-Neanderthal, Cro-Magnon wonders that we are, who destroy every admirable thing we make and corrupt every beautiful thing we see, yet each one of us is the firstborn of the world, touching the earth for the first time, speaking the first word, taking the first step toward wherever our steps take us.

We know what the last step will be. But what happens between first and last is basically up for grabs—a strange stew of destiny and decisions—a whole lot of monkey-see, monkey-do mixed in with the possibility, the threat, of monkey climb down from the tree and create the Sistine Chapel. Or the Holocaust. Take your pick.

Is this why life is so serious, why what we do and say and become is so . . . so *real*?

The world hangs on a string, like a bead strung between empty space and the blazing heart of the sun, and the string tightens and the world starts to spin and suddenly we're here! Laughing, dancing, crumbling away and dying, but here, now, here I am!

I praise you and bow to you, God of making and unmaking, for creating and not creating this universe where you are known and unknown, absent and immanent—this place that sleeps yet sees—this living dynamic fertile cornucopic biomorphic solid immovable static empty voidness that will never bend to my will—but is always supple, responsive, clay under my fingers.

It is wrong, wrong, wrong to put God in the past tense. Better to say, God loves—the world—loves us, its imperfect, searching, foolish, magnificent offspring, so much that instead of waving a magic wand, he takes us on a journey into unknown territory, giving the gifts of his guidance and love in mystery and deep silence, so we are free to live and become something that wasn't here before and will never be here again—and again, and again. No beginning. No end.

Is this why our existence is so terrifying, so beautiful? Because whatever we do here, the first and last requirement is that it must be honest? Lives hang in the balance, and we don't know how the story will end? Our own story? Everyone's story?

I see the world, and I ask why? Why would a benevolent god stir my soul with the beauty of a blade of grass, in a world where there is so much suffering, so much horror? Why?

Questions, questions, always the questions . . . Try to look at it from another direction. We think of benevolence like newborn rabbits seeking warmth and safety. We think the harbor is the best place to be, when the big wide ocean is calling. We want a God who protects and comforts, but what if God wants us to live out our own story as far and as long as our imagination and sense of adventure will take us?

Seems like a whole lot of wasted effort if what we do here is not the real thing. So why not dive in and make something out of it? The last judgment, maybe the only judgment of a lived life is: "Look at what you missed, you dumb cluck! What you needed was so simple, right in front of you, if you had your eyes open."

Benevolence. That's what it comes down to. How would a truly benevolent god behave?

But look at me now, pretending like I understand the mind of God. What a jerk.

You know, with all this ranting and whining, I forgot to say hello. Hi there. My name is Brian. Glad our paths have crossed. Sit down, take the load off your feet, and tell me a story—your story. I'll tell you mine. Maybe we'll learn something that will help us on our journeys. Worth a try.

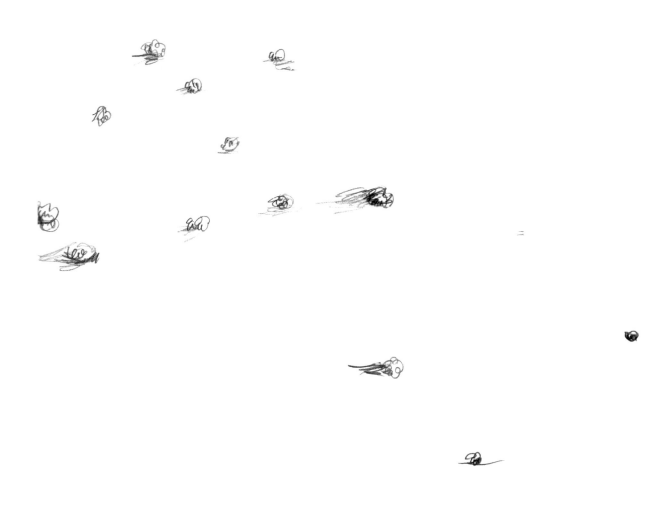

How Am I Doing?

Susan was busy. Always busy. She had books to read, papers to write, classes to attend. She was walking the walk and talking the talk. Literally talking the talk. She spoke the language. Me, her head-case, tagalong husband—I walked. Tried to learn a few words before I made the trip to Germany. An average two-year-old left me in the linguistic dust.

I was walking on a gravel path near the university one day, minding my own business, when a shiny black Mercedes jerked out of traffic and stopped right in front of me. Door opened. German dude got out, business suit minus jacket, marched up to me in a few strides, and proceeded with the *Deutsch sprechen* routine. He pointed at a street sign then turned and pointed in the direction his car was going, waved his hands wildly, and I finally figured out that he wanted some help getting where he was going.

I knew enough German to appreciate the elegant sentence structure as it unfolded—how they bob and weave their way through a chain of words, gathering steam with adjectives and adverbs and God knows what else, always making sure to use the right endings so the organization is clear, until finally, with every brick in place, out pops the perfect verb form that ties it all together. And then that faint smile of satisfaction that says, Now that's whatcha call a sentence, job well done.

I waited patiently while Mercedes guy spun out his complex web of ordered sound. When he was done, I shrugged my shoulders and said, "*Ich spreche kein Deutsch.*"

Mercedes dude's jaw froze, he raised his eyebrows, and looked me up and down as if I'd just turned into a department store mannequin. "Ahhhh," he replied, then performed an abrupt about-face, walked briskly back to his car, and sped away.

I guess it was the beard. They all thought I was German. That was a problem when somebody needed directions, but it helped me out on the trains. Even better, I had figured out that if I changed one number on my train pass, I could eke out a few extra weeks unencumbered by the need for a ticket.

German conductors were imposing fellows, with their black uniforms and official-looking hats. When they opened the door to the train car, stepped in with a flourish, and announced "*Bitte die Fahrkarten,*" you knew they meant business. But all I had to do was sit there and look German, then wave my doctored train pass in their faces, and they would sniff and move on.

Susan was busy being a high-powered philosophy student at the University of Hamburg. I was busy falling apart. Actually I had already fallen apart before she left for Germany. As had our marriage, more or less. Whether or not either could be put back together again—uncertain at best.

I'd moved from Montana to Philadelphia to learn how to write music at the mecca of music schools for composers, the University of Pennsylvania. After barely a year, I stopped going to classes, stopped doing anything remotely creative, and started selling cameras at a department store for a buck and a quarter an hour.

Instead of mapping out my future and pulling together the most impressive résumé imaginable, I spent my days wandering through the woods and my nights adding to a growing pile of notebooks full of dreams, sketches, mandalas, and doodles.

Imagine a vast field of sea grass, waving in warm currents, bathed in muted sunlight. Suddenly a hand breaks the water, yanks out a single blade of grass, and buries it in desert sand. How would that blade of sea grass feel? Or imagine a flock of geese, flying in formation toward the rising sun. A hunter fires from below and a single goose drops to the ground, wing broken, unable to fly. How would that goose feel as he watched the rest of the flock disappear?

Other than a couple of loyal college comrades, dreams were the best friends I had in those years. As with most other events in my life, I had a dream that seemed to explain what was going on: I was seated in a meditative position, my knees under me, in outer space somewhere near the earth, calmly receiving the warmth of the sun. Suddenly a net appeared, like a fishing net that encircled the sun, then something pulled it away and I was in total darkness. The dream ended with an image of me, sitting alone on the surface of the moon, trying to decipher strange symbols that appeared nearby in the dry dust.

We are all nourished and sustained by an invisible connection with—something—so much a part of us that we're completely unaware of its existence. It was my fate to be made aware, through its absence.

I was a college dropout. A failure. My wife had left for Europe, I had alienated my family, and most of my friends had moved on to PhD programs and jobs. Me—I was working on the eighth floor of Wanamaker's selling Instamatics to little old ladies and traveling on a mythic journey to the underworld.

I was also like a miner trapped underground whose brain was foggy from lack of oxygen, who could no longer tell which way was up.

The plan was for Susan to go to Hamburg while I worked a couple of jobs and saved enough money to join her for a few months. Then she would come back after a year and we'd live happily ever after. That was the plan. The "me joining her" part worked out fine. The "her coming back" part, *nicht so gut*. But that's another story.

Like I said, Susan was a busy philosophy student, and I had those extra weeks on my train pass. So to entertain myself, I took train rides. I remembered my grandfather uttering one of the few words of Swedish he knew: *Yo-ta-bor-hey*. He loved to savor that word, rolling it out in a deep basso profundo, probably imitating his father who'd landed in Brooklyn from the old country. *Yo-ta-bor-hey*—Göteborg—Gothenburg—the ancestral home. I had time to kill, so why not go see what he was talking about?

I spent several days there, by myself, wandering around and seeing what I had eyes to see. Which was lots of very tall people with long hair, sometimes in business suits. Friendly enough— but formidable. I developed a new appreciation for the poor saps who had the bad luck to be living on the coast in the north of England and Ireland, you know, back in the day. One of those elegant Viking longboats appears on the horizon, and it's time to head for the hills.

I also saw stones. That's what I remember about the place that shaped my grandfather's DNA. Stones by the sea—jagged, bare, thrusting into the air like rows of sharpened teeth. Strange, very strange. I'd seen those stones before.

What a hopeless cliché, I thought. But there it was—familiarity. I knew those stones. I can't explain it. I just knew them.

All those big beautiful Swedes—how did they shoehorn themselves into such an array of tiny cars? There wasn't a car to be seen bigger than a matchbox. Rush hour in Göteborg was like a go-kart convention. Which made the '50s-era Ford station wagon filled with long-haired, besotted young Vikings hard to miss.

Now *that* was a vehicle. Easily twenty feet long, pure white, with big fins in the back and a massive V-8 engine that conjured up a raging T-Rex downing primordial mammals in a single bite.

Hey, it was Friday night, and what's a young Beowulf-in-training to do with all that pent-up raping and pillaging energy? These guys piloted their war schooner through the streets of Göteborg, and when they spotted somebody strolling down the sidewalk, they'd lower the windows, stick their hairy crania into the evening breeze, and out would come a chorus of the most fearsome Viking yells that their barely civilized psyches could conjure up. Sure enough, they finally spotted me, and the choir executed a perfect primeval roar with my name on it. I felt the bloodlust stir in my repressed poetic soul: Brothers of Odin, sharpen your spears, to war! There are heads to be cracked, a world to be conquered!

But my comrades-in-arms had already turned a corner and disappeared. Me—I kept on walking.

When I got back to Hamburg, Susan told me that my mother had called—a big deal in those days. A transatlantic phone call. While I'd been conjuring up ancient bloodlusts on the auld sod, my Yo-ta-bor-hay grandfather had died. I'd missed his funeral while visiting the graves of his ancestors. I felt an odd chill travel up and down my spine when I heard that.

A few days later I decided to go to Bremerhaven, a little shore town about an hour from Hamburg. I wanted to walk by the ocean. So I did. As I walked, I thought of a dream I'd had years earlier; in the dream I was walking by the ocean and a magic gold coin had washed up, and I found the coin.

I walked along the beach near Bremerhaven, waves crashing in and slithering out, head down, studying the shoreline detritus. I knew I would find something important. Had to be that coin….

Suddenly I tripped and nearly fell in the wet sand. What I'd tripped on was a bird, lying on its side, a bird with a long neck, a big white bird, or at least once it was white. Now its feathers were dirty, where it had any feathers left.

What would a swan be doing on the wintry shores of the North Atlantic? I had no idea.

I began to feel like I was inside a dream, gazing at myself. I was looking for magic but found a dying swan, so far gone that all it could do was raise its head and look at me with an unblinking eye. I stood there for at least an hour, shivering, and watched it die.

Cold. I was cold. Inside. Cold that drained away movement, sucked away energy. Cold that bathed the whole world in translucent blue, separating one color from another, one object from another, with crystalline clarity. There was nothing more beautiful than that clarifying light. And nothing more tempting, more dangerous to a wanderer like me.

The dreams still flowed in great torrents. The daily movements of the interior tides—the openings and closings, inhales and exhales—were as predictable as the tap of a wave on the pylon of a pier that jutted into a vast sea. The fire still burned in the furnace, and every day I turned toward that fire, knelt before it, warmed my hands in its steady heat.

Nothing had changed. Except a year or two had gone by since the door opened and I stepped into this otherworldly landscape. Time had gone by in the slow drip of days, and yes, nothing had changed. For that very reason, everything had changed. But the transition was so slow and so imperceptible that to the one who experienced it, there was no change, except for the ripening of a succulent fruit that would soon be plucked and eaten.

All this was happening to me. All this had been given to me. I, me, this one here, the one who'd gone from promising young creative wunderkind to dreamer who spent long winter afternoons in sunny cemeteries watching the light pour down on the earth through cracks in the clouds. The one who, back in Philadelphia, had put on his pathetic blue polyester suit, sat on the underground trolley looking at his reflection in the dark window, and punched the time clock in the basement of Wanamaker's department store.

The one who was existing in the world but who'd dismantled every bridge to the world. The one who might just as well have been one of those burned-out derelicts huddling on street corners and sleeping in alleys, who saw things that weren't there and said things to people who didn't exist.

But I knew, or thought I knew, that I was blessed. I had seen and known what few had seen and known. I was beloved of God, I thought. How else to explain the complete strangeness of my life, the unasked-for gifts, the visions of light, all of it, everything—how else to explain?

All this had happened, and continued to happen, and would always happen, I thought. This, now, was my life, and it was a good life.

And so a subtle hubris had crept in, a confidence born of dreams and the inward journey, but the confidence of a mesmerized sailor whose sailboat drifted in an endless, beautiful sea.

Years earlier I'd made a photograph of light shining through a crack underneath a door. The image represented hope to me in a time when my life was falling apart. Someday I will go through that door, I said to myself, and in that place of light I will discover my life and my creativity.

A few days after the Bremerhaven trip, I saw the door again in a dream, with a dazzling light pouring between door and floor. I was moving slowly, steadily toward the door, but instead of joy at the prospect of opening the door and bathing in the light, I felt abject terror, as if a terrible mistake was about to happen and there was nothing I could do about it. My father was calling me to come back, not to go there, it was the wrong time, I had a life to live first. As I woke up, I'd almost reached the door, and I was shaken, trembling with terror.

That's when I *felt* the cold, felt its icy tentacles penetrating my body. That's when I finally *saw* how deeply I'd sunken into myself. I had gone as far as I could go toward that light and still come back. To go further would be to allow myself to be seduced, to be turned aside from the purpose of all that had happened, which was to *live*.

Like Jonah, I'd been to the belly of the beast, then was spit out on the shore. But not just to go my merry way. There was work to be done.

Look at a map of a typical German city, and you'll see a tapestry of green splotches scattered throughout, each one with a name, usually some long-dead hero of art, science, politics, or war. Something mysterious and ancient in the German soul lurks in those parks, something deep in the earth where the blind roots slowly sniff their way toward the druidic springs, the old world where spirits and faeries inhabited every brook and tree, and gods and heroes strolled through the earthly realm.

A few days before I left Germany, I decided to take one last walk through my favorite park. A storm had just begun to clear—the sun, glimpsed here and there through the clouds. My feet took me to a place I'd never been before, and I walked along quietly, head down, thinking. Suddenly, in a clearing, I stumbled on a huge monolith—almost like a pyramid, with steps on all four sides, leading up to a flat place on the top where perhaps you could look around and, instead of seeing the modern city, imagine a dark green forest stretched to the horizon.

On a whim I ran up the steps, and just as I reached the top, the sun broke through the clouds, pouring down on the world, bathing everything in clear yellow light. I was cold no longer! I could feel the warmth of that light working its way down into my sinews. I opened my arms to the sky and the light, and for the first time in years I felt the animal joy of the living organism, grateful for every vibrating molecule of my body, grateful for the smell of the fresh breeze after the clearing storm.

Later that day I watched the sunset through a window in the kitchen of Susan's dormitory, and I felt a presence, a consciousness inside me—a silent fatherly voice that spoke to me in its very silence, a silence that said, I am here, child, I am here, with you. I am here.

I stopped, listened, slowly found my own silence and said, "Thank you, Father. I am leaving now. Leaving to do my best to give back what I've seen. Such gifts. Such gifts."

Suddenly a kind of sweet, terrible anguish welled up inside, and I turned toward the voice and said, "How am I doing? Could I have done more with what I was given? Have I held back, or have I lived a full measure? How am I doing?"

It was not the yearning of a child wanting to please a stern parent. It was just an honest seeker, one more voice in the multitude, who wanted to know the truth.

How am I doing? Ask that question and mean it when you ask, ask it without words, ask it every day with all your strength and all your heart, and chances are you'll find what you need, get to where you must go.

Almost as an afterthought, the next day, a few answering words in silence, inside. "Live. Nothing else. Just live." And so I have. And so I have.

Sea of Light #45, 2013

I Give My Eyes

At dusk, a deer in the yard, a doe. She stands, silently, for several minutes, alert, wary, sniffing and tasting the cold air, waiting, listening.

Suddenly she moves. Head down. Nibble of dead grass. Head up, eyes forward, then sideways. Ears twitch. Head down again. Nibble of dead grass. Another nibble. Nose up high in the air, then again, down.

Three big bites of brown crabgrass.

She steps forward, eyes wide, testing the wind. Then, head down again, more nibbles, steps, sniffs, and bites. More sniffs, twitches, ups and downs, over and over, never the same, always repeating but nothing the same—she is both a ballerina and a blade of grass in a gentle breeze, moving in a precise, rhythmic, intelligently unintentional dance of perfectly choreographed line and form.

"What's going on out there?" Helen comes up quietly behind me, sees the deer through the back porch window, stops.

"Are we this beautiful too?" I ask, turning toward her. "You know, people"—I point to myself—"us."

She scans my frame from head to toe, scratches her chin, smiles. "Maybe it depends on who's looking," she says over her shoulder as she walks back into the kitchen.

The deer moves, and with every step a perfectly sculpted form disappears while another blossoms before my eyes, *buddingdyingbloomingbudding*, no way to tease them apart, yet each, coalescing briefly, leaves me breathless for the next.

The deer moves, and she is mortal flesh and eternal moments of grace, a living archetype of the ordinary beauty folded into every vibrating molecule in the known and undiscovered cosmos.

The deer moves, and my eyes are two periscopes raised up from deep waters, surveying creation with curiosity and delight.

Yes, I answer my own question, we're as beautiful as the deer, we are, we all bear the stamp, the mark of the maker, the beauty is in us, in everything, we just have to stop blocking the periscope.

We need to step aside and let what's in out, and what's *out* in.

"If only . . . you could see . . . how beautiful you are . . . to me," croons the maker's mark in our cells, in our souls.

For twenty years deer have roamed through the backyard, invading my garden, stripping bark from favorite trees. Deer are as common, and as welcome, as ants at a picnic.

But that doe, that day, is a messenger, and this is the message she brings: Every living thing has the mark of the maker in its molecules, and can't help but be beautiful. And who would make something beautiful and then not love what had been made?

The world is full of horror and terror and mayhem and random death. It's the way things are, maybe even the way things need to be. Still, the deer walks in beauty. Not knowing. Being.

But today I see her beauty, and know it in myself.

To observe and to be the thing observed—to hammer the nail home, right hand not knowing what the left hand is doing. This is what I've been looking for, as long as I can remember: To open my eyes, then get out of the way and let the dance begin.

That evening, my wife told me I stood like a statue for a half hour, maybe more, watching the doe move through our yard. The look on Helen's face said, C'mon, tell me, what were you seeing?

I didn't know what to say. I'd seen it before, but never so clearly, so simply—that stamp of beauty—the maker's mark.

"I gave my eyes to God today." The words sounded hollow, disembodied. I glanced at Helen, shrugged my shoulders in mock defeat.

But that was my answer to her silent question. I wasn't sure why those words came to me, or what they meant, but there they were again, wanting a second chance, another dance. This time they almost felt—real.

"I give my eyes to God."

Life Forms #53, 1990

River of Dream

The earliest one was about the river. I didn't *remember* it until many years later. Maybe *remember* isn't the right word, because *remember* might make you think the river was real, made of moving water and fish and bugs and black earth beneath it all.

Water, yes, there was water, big and warm, and it flowed like a slow watery glacier of liquid light toward some faraway magical place that was always there but too far away to touch or see. I couldn't imagine anything more beautiful. Standing by that river, I knew the whole world was made of warmth and glow and shimmer and shine and happy, yes, but peaceful, quiet happy, not all jokey and cheerful. This was different. This was the River of Dream.

No sign of fish. A fish couldn't breathe in that water. But the river was real, more real than anything fingers could touch and eyes could see.

I dreamed about that river and walked beside it before I could walk and maybe even before I knew what a river was. At least it felt that way when I remembered the dream many years later, when I was as alone as I've ever been. Camping and hiking in the Montana mountains, no one but me and my fishing pole and backpack and dreams dredged up from an unknown well whose water filled me with remembering, places and stories long forgotten.

Four days, alone in the wilderness, and the dreams, the dreams—detailed, rich with image and memory, they took page after page in my journal. I spent half of each day recording dreams, the other half fishing. The journal sits in a box somewhere. I could find it. But I'd rather look elsewhere for what remains, trust the more elusive precision of memory.

When I search my remembering of those four solitary days, I find the dream about the little town by the sea:

A peaceful town flourishes by the sea, doing the work that little towns do. Everyone who lives there has a job that's important to the town's survival, and what each person does is part of what makes the town a town. So who it is and what it does are the same little song that the town sings every day to itself, and to the waters, and to the wind in the air. Everything is peaceful in the town because towns are supposed to be that way, aren't they? There's nothing unusual about a peaceful little town by the sea.

Then one day the ships appear, big dark ships from far away, and the ships sit silently watching the little town do its work, sing its song. Suddenly guns in the ships begin to fire on the town, and once they start, they never stop, whole flotillas of ships with guns pointing at the town, firing without mercy, day after day, gradually breaking the walls that protect the town and destroying streets and houses. There is too much damage to fix what is broken. Finally when the soldiers come, the people do what the soldiers want them to do. Smile. All the time. Smile. C'mon now, the soldiers say, let's see some tooth in that grin. At first it's hard, all that smiling, but soon the town forgets what it's like to be a town. So life goes on, day after day. But the sea hears no singing from the town anymore.

I woke up in my tent, crawled out of my sleeping bag, built up the fire, boiled some water, cleaned a couple of brook trout that I'd caught the day before, dipped them in flour and dropped them in the aluminum skillet, then mixed up some oatmeal, and soon my cells were happy knowing they'd be cells for another day. And all the while that dream of the town was bouncing around my skull. Its simple metaphor of home, invasion and occupation, desired behavior enforced through violence and fear—the dream was a gift. The gift was clarity.

I knew what had happened to me long ago. I saw what had sculpted my angles and curves, pounded the rivets, and tightened the screws.

In the dark canyons of ancient memory where a soul's secrets are hidden, a door had opened and light was pouring in.

My mother and father were decent folks who did their best with the tools they were given. They went about the parenting thing the way it was done to them. There was nothing "wrong" with how my parents raised their children, no out-of-the-ordinary physical stuff, no dark secrets other than an above-average dose of that Greek fella Mr. Oedipus.

My parents did what they believed would produce civilized children. They did it without questioning its wisdom, even, at times, with unnecessary enthusiasm. But they didn't hurt their kids because they enjoyed it. I recall my mother even uttering the classic "hurts me more than you" cliché while administering corporal punishment, and I think she meant it. That which offends in a child must be removed. How? Attack unacceptable behavior, do it every day, every opportunity. Like the ships firing on the little town by the sea, attack—with words, with emotional violence, and if necessary, with ritualized physical violence.

I saw the result in another dream, remembered, from the solitude of the mountains:

A boy, walking toward me, nicely dressed, plucked from a drawer labeled Ideal American Child, smiling like a Boy Scout in a Norman Rockwell magazine cover. As he gets nearer, I begin to see what he can't: his body has split, front side the perfect child, but behind, beyond his vision, an angry monster, a male Medusa with tentacles instead of hair, face contorted with silent pain and rage, chained but struggling to be released from his cruel prison.

Why am I bringing up these parental crimes and misdemeanors committed by hardworking and productive people who did their best, whose mistakes grew out of their own traumas? Because it's the only way to explain where I found myself as I entered adult life. I was Jekyll and Hyde, Inc.: in a constant state of interior warfare, a war made worse because it was beyond the reach of consciousness, like a giant taproot growing down into the deepest soil, before there was a "me" there to observe, ponder, and resist.

Of all the youthful memories, which are the burrs under the saddle? Which ones persist, demanding to be heard? The Mendelssohn overture. And the sad look on the pianist's face—yes, the older lady at the Red Lion Bar and Restaurant. She was part of a jazz trio that played on Friday nights. The bass player was a friend of a friend, a pilot by profession, but trained as a composer. The reed man was my high school orchestra conductor, and the jazz piano lady—she was the star.

It took about twenty-five minutes to walk home from school. Just about right for a couple repetitions of the Mendelssohn overture that was named after a cave. Fingal's Cave. I'd never even been inside a cave, and had no idea why the composer was so interested in that one. But I was in the high school orchestra now, and this was the first big-league piece of music I heard from the inside. No more kid's stuff—the real thing. I was so stirred by the experience that I memorized the entire viola part, note for note, and quietly hummed it to myself as I walked.

I was falling in love with music, yes, but even more with the people who wrote and played it. These were my people. They had what I wanted. The jazz trio—they had it too, and I could talk to them, learn from them!

Friday nights I drove my parents' brown Buick station wagon down to the Red Lion, found a table near the musicians, and listened to them play jazz standards. I learned the rituals of jazz— the spots where you're supposed to be quiet, where you applaud, where it's okay to shout a couple encouraging words. I picked up a few basics about how music is put together. *This is where we start, how far can we travel, and how will we get back home again?* That's the story of most jazz improvs.

Mainly the jazz lady taught me how much joy a person could feel just being a person. The way her hands moved, her head bounced, her feet tapped the pedals—her whole face lit up—

the banging and rippling of keys and chords. It all said, what a gas it is to be alive!

I saw my life clearly. What I wanted—it was serious. Like the Mendelssohn overture was serious, and the jazz trio. Finding that quality myself would take commitment. It was time to dive in.

I dropped out of every club, governing body, and extracurricular activity, and began to write music in my spare time. Studied with the viola player who'd studied with the famous composer at the university, and these guys, their world, became my world. What they had, I was hungry for. I didn't have a name for it. Something so simple it was easy to miss, but try to possess it and the very act of trying took you further away.

These musicians liked who they were—the whole package, not just the nice parts you're supposed to like. They had sensitivities of eye and ear far beyond mine, yet their ability to listen did not make them soft, undisciplined. What they created had a soul to it, an inner beauty. In learning how to sing their own song, they had somehow been healed of the warfare I felt in myself.

I wanted what they had and knew I was a million miles from getting it. I was nothing. A klutz. A fool. A bumbling idiot. A zero. A living lie. Everything I said, every move I made, was unreal. There was no truth in me. No roots. None.

Was I too hard on myself? No. No. I was simply being honest. Through the music I heard, the people I met who played it, and especially the minds and innards of those questing, soaring souls who wrote it, I began to see the truth about myself.

I was broken. I had to heal myself. Or be healed. Those people had done it. If they did, I could too. There had to be a way. If there was I would find it.

So I set to work. I enrolled at the university so I could study with the famous guy and discovered that like most artists he was nowhere near as famous as he wanted or deserved to be. But he was kind to me, and I learned more from him than probably any other teacher. I spent all day at the music department, and when I went back to my dorm room I sat down at the little desk in the corner and copied music, because I wanted to learn how to make a musical score look beautiful. My nickname in the dorm was "Screaming Mozart Idiot."

But after a year my teacher retired and went away so I studied again with the viola player (who was also a composer), but I knew I had to go away myself, and soon, or I would die, or at least my soul would die, and is there any difference?

I wrote music, heard it played, wrote more music. Sometimes my compositions would start with something beautiful, about to be born. But the idea never worked out, never got off the ground. Imagine Old Faithful rising in the sunlight, then fizzling in a few seconds, never hitting its stride, never finding its rhythm. Then it dries up, goes away.

I decided to stop trying so hard, to stop thinking about the proper order of the black spots of ink on the page, and just write, let what happens happen.

So I wrote a piece for violin and viola, and my teacher and his wife learned it, and we rented a big theater in the middle of town and organized a concert, and lots of people came, and who did I see in the audience but the piano jazz lady from the Red Lion! She had come to hear my music. I was happy. Proud.

They played the piece, and afterward I went out into the theater, and there she was, but instead of a smile, she looked at me with a terrible sad look of pity and almost horror. She said little. I don't remember the words, but I heard the piece through her ears, and what she perceived was the truth. Oh you poor boy, she said, more or less. I had no idea how you're suffering, she said, how much pain you have. I am so sad for you, she said, so sad.

She was not criticizing me. She felt it. Felt my sorrow and emptiness and the warfare inside and how my real music was stuck in there and couldn't get out. And it was true. I knew it. True.

God, my God, oh my God, oh my . . .

God. I hate that word. It's like trying to thread a needle with a drainpipe, or using a thimble to drink an ocean.

A word is a box that encloses a bunch of smaller cartons, bottles, and storage bags, each with various things inside them. What those containers inside the word box look like, what they contain and how they all fit together, is kind of, sort of, generally, and approximately grooved on and more or less agreed upon by nearly everybody. So when a person says "chrysanthemum," all the bottles and cartons inside the chrysanthemum word box contain the same basic stuff and fit together more or less the same way for almost everyone, so those four syllables of sound symbolize the same thing in our advanced mammalian brains.

Words flow into other words and new words are born as new ways to share what life dishes out are needed. If enough people decide a word stands for something real, it's like a freight train. No one can stop it because people like the feel of the word on the tongue.

But sometimes we use the same word in so many different ways that its box gets jam-packed with random junk and it stops being useful as a way to express shared experience.

The word box labeled God has become an aromatic landfill of cans, bottles, plastic bags, and disposable cardboard boxes full of yet more non-recyclable detritus tossed in from every branch and tributary of human history. Many people have claimed that their God word boxes are the correct ones, the only ones, and untold millions have killed and/or been killed for no other reason than the fear that their God word boxes might be polluted by somebody else's.

Now is that the stupidest thing you've ever heard of, or what? Kill somebody because they have a different slant on something so big and unknowable that nobody has any hope of ever getting anywhere near understanding what it is, or even if?

Wouldn't there be at least as much entertainment in finding out how another person sees things? You know, compare and contrast, maybe learn something? Unless people really enjoy killing each other and are just waiting for the right excuse to come along. But that can't be true . . .

This sharing instead of murdering concept—I'll begin by attempting to clear out the cobwebs in my *own* God word box and seeing what's in there after roughly sixty-three years of roaming the earth:

God is Dream. I had no interest in God until the dreams arrived, bringing with them something bigger, deeper, wiser, older, and in every way more God-like than me. The dreams came because—but I don't know where they came from or why, except I knew what I wanted and eventually learned how to get down on my knees and ask for it.

I'd moved from Missoula, Montana, to Philadelphia, had become a genuine card-carrying Ivy Leaguer, and was part of a thriving community of serious musicians—a whole gang of screaming Mozart idiots. I'd learned to mask my failures with greater sophistication, but nothing had changed. The creative river had a damp place here and there but generally was desert dry. I put those black dots on the blank paper, but they weren't, somehow, necessary. Instead of leaping into song, they were dead on the page.

One of my teachers said what was missing in my work was "interior dialogue." It was another way of saying, there's darkness in there where there should be light. There's a missing ingredient, a plug that's been pulled out, a dance with no dance partner.

I am sick and must be healed. I never spoke those words, to myself or anyone, but I felt their truth in ways that no words could ever describe. No amount of hard work could fix what ailed me. My problem was more basic. That internal dialogue—the light inside that I saw in people all around me—this was what the piano lady was looking for at that painful moment of truth.

I was desperate. Because I understood, finally, that I couldn't solve this problem by intelligent, purposeful application of force.

Was my life going to be a slowly withering falsehood? How do you find the truth, not some fact or theorem, but the deep flowing waters of living creative energy that join you with the world and its beauty and pain? Do you find that "truth," or does it find you?

The word *conversion* does not mean "pound people over the head until they think the way I do." It originally meant a moment of turning, when out of necessity a new direction opens up in a person's life. Now I can see that this period of desperation was also my time of turning, my "conversion." I was reaching out, imploring.

In ancient terms, I was kneeling at the altar of Athena or Apollo and offering ritual sacrifice. I was a bereft Psalmist crying out to the heavens for the divine voice inside that could no longer be heard. I was the despised tax collector in the Gospels, rending his clothes, beating his chest, and crying wordlessly, "God have mercy."

I had, after many struggles and much failure, reached a place where there was nothing left but my small naked soul and the emptiness within, and the certainty that I would never find what I hungered for on my own. I needed help. But from where, by whom?

I wouldn't have remotely called it by this name back then, in fact would have been offended by the word, but this moment was the beginning of prayer. Not the "can I have more or less of this or that" prayer, no, more like the Psalm with that rumbling Latin phrase at the beginning: *De profundis clamavi.* Out of the depths I cry unto you, my God, oh my God.

You can't fake it with your soul. You may think you can, but somewhere in there an honest pair of eyes and ears sees and hears, and speaks what it knows in its own way, on its own timetable. Finally, I was learning to listen.

Then the dam burst, and the dreams came pouring out. And oh my God what dreams, what dreams.

Later I numbered them. Number one was simple, just an image of a man, me, swimming at night, in the ocean, toward a full moon, and a feeling of peace, mystery.

The second one was scary but hopeful. I throw an apple at a neighbor's door, it awakens a terrifying mother who chases after me and wants to kill me, I run and hide while a father-like dude talks to her and calms her down.

There was another one that painted a grim picture of the state of my soul: I was a child in a grocery store, wandering from aisle to aisle looking for candy, ignoring the really nourishing stuff on all the aisles easily within my reach.

But the main one, the powerful one, is always there in my remembering place, strong and steady. It was about a journey downward, through twists and turns, down steps, to a beautiful pool invisible from the house where the path began. The goal was to swim in the pool, which was a kind of baptism, a place of healing, where people who swam were joined together. First I made the journey with a young woman. The way down was dangerous, but we made it, and we swam in the pool. Then I led a larger group of people down the same path, and it was a more difficult journey, but we also arrived and swam in the pool. Before I left the place, I stood for a while, drinking in its sacred beauty.

Oh my remembering God, what those first few dreams did to me, how they turned me around and turned my world upside down and inside out. They were priceless gifts. Each one rich with symbolic wisdom yet brutally honest, a call to arms. And the main one telling a beautiful story of passage, baptism, healing, and union.

A door had opened, but where had I been and where was I going? Wherever it was, I felt like a grasshopper peering over the edge of the Grand Canyon. *But still,* I thought, *I had wings, and I could fly.*

This was the path to the place where I wanted to be. I knew it. I was the desert wanderer looking for an oasis who instead stumbled onto the seashore and found a fully provisioned one-person yacht with a sign that said: *Climb aboard and start sailing, no experience necessary.*
And in the fine print: *Keep the buckets and life vests handy.*

God is Dream. Yes. But Dream is empty air unless it's making, becoming something. God is the seed in the soil. *Possibility.* My own private God word box has plenty of Dream inside; let's throw in a jar of Growing. I bow to the God of things that grow. Not only things I can grasp and see, but especially growing on the inside, where the stakes are higher.

So I went on a journey. A journey of Dream.

I recall those early days with a grim smile. I believed the journey would be a pleasant working vacation, like a visit to the Dream Doctor's Spa and Rehab Center, where I'd get a Mythological Mud Bath and maybe a Psychic Soul Massage, then be back in time to polish off my music history classes and head home for the holidays.

But I was walking a new and dangerous path without guide, map, or compass.

Now I see the "me" that grew from that journey. But then, when it all began, I only had the dreams and an instinct that I could trust where they were taking me.

From the outside looking in, I was lost in a world of fantasy, with delusions about some hypothetical transformation of the soul, while in reality I was rapidly losing everything respectable and credible—money, marriage, education, future. It was four years before I hit the bottom of the well, and five before I was functional enough to pick up the pieces of a busted-up life, then go back to school and atone for my F's and Incompletes and No Reports.

Depression—was that what ailed me? I suppose it was that terrifying condition we call depression, at times—but no, that word does not explain it. The dreams, and what was in the dreams: their intense creativity and complex symbolic language, filled with stuff that was so far above my minimum-wage soul pay grade that even now, with nearly a lifetime to consider and search, the questions haven't changed. What are the origins, the roots of such experiences?

Why did this happen to me, an ordinary middle-class kid from Montana whose parents were not exactly dream-weaving shamans muttering incantations and talking to obscure gods? Au contraire. They were scientists and teachers, people of logic and the mind, who thought of religion and the soul as pleasant diversions from the real work of life.

So there I was, the son of hardworking practical people, and instead of building a life I was sitting in the woods recording dreams as if they were gospel, drawing crude little pictures of tunnels of light stretching from my head to the sun, and in general acting like a mushroom eater or an acid freak (I wasn't) or a delusional madman (still not entirely sure).

Eventually I began to draw mandalas that corresponded to things I saw or instincts about where this adventure had taken me so far. One day I woke up and in my mind's eye, suddenly all the universe was a flowing stream of beautiful geometry that wove into and out of the center of a mandala that was also an egg. I spent hours with a compass and ruler, drawing a single moment of this endless flow of geometrical perfection. I wrote a simple poem that tries to describe the intense mystery of the moment, which felt like a curtain being opened to a deeper, more fundamental reality:

Eternal Oneness
Original Unity

Everywhere
Circles, triangles, squares
I close my eyes and they are there.

In and out, up and down,
Back and forth, all around,
Moving, shifting, blending, flowing,
Always crossing, never slowing.
Close your eyes and they are there.

A decade later I learned that the medieval priests who dreamed up the Gothic cathedrals saw something similar and wove subtle geometries into their transcendental architecture. They called it God. All I knew was that I needed a handhold, an affirmation that wherever I was headed, I wasn't on a path to oblivion.

The mandalas became more and more intricate, partly because I'd stopped going to classes and had endless time to tinker with the details. I was proud of these drawings—even foolishly thought of them as works of art. I believed then—and still believe—that they were emblems or markers

Mandala, 1976

that reflected the stages of the healing process that was going on in my soul.

I was aware of how this mumbo-jumbo looked to others, but I had to follow where I was led. The stakes were about as high as you can get—a soul, a life—*my* life. Things were falling apart on the outside, but I was still alive *inside*. And I never knew on a given day what fresh magic might pop out of the dream-oven.

Occasionally the oven door even opened when the sun was up—like that summer afternoon when I rode my bike to the park and hiked to a secluded spot where I could be completely alone for a few hours, absorbing the life of the forest and watching the light flashing on the creek far below.

I sat there, as I always did, reading, sleeping, writing in my journal. Suddenly, a one-two-three punch: jab—cross—jab. Three big "waking dreams." Images, ideas, symbols—not sure what to call them—but they took over, for a few minutes. Uninvited. But still is a source of wonder and contemplation.

First: *An image of a man sitting with legs crossed in the center of a square room, empty, with a single window. He meditates contentedly as a soft, diffuse light permeates the room. Then the man raises his head, looks at the window, and an intense sunbeam fills the room, enveloping him in radiant luminosity.*

A few years earlier I'd read a book by William Butler Yeats called *A Vision*, which tells the strange story of a "visitation": his wife began to go into trances and write stuff down that, like my dreams, was filled with sophisticated and arcane knowledge. Yeats quickly concluded that this "automatic writing" was an attempt at communication from druidic spirits, who wanted to reveal ancient secrets about cycles of history and the nature of the afterlife—things a respectable Irish poet needed to have in his toolkit. Toward the end of the experience, Yeats point-blank asked these spirits why they were doing this, and why he was the lucky recipient. They replied, "To give you metaphors for poetry."

I had thought of myself as a freak. While everybody else was going about their daily lives, and my friends were graduating, moving on, getting advanced degrees, building lives, what was I doing? Wandering in the woods seeing lovely visions of eternal light, meanwhile becoming a complete failure at all the tasks a young person is expected to accomplish.

But my innards were telling me a different story. Maybe everyone, aware of it or not, is fed by the invisible light that flows into our souls. Maybe I wasn't a freak, I'd just learned how to open up the windows and pull back the curtains and let more sunlight in the room. Maybe my own list of "metaphors for poetry" would begin and end with light.

Second: *An image of a man positioned high above the earth in empty space, standing on a vast, infinitely extended plane made of a clear material that is still solid. The man stands with one foot on each side of a line that marks a balancing point. He must keep the plane level and steady. Every thought, every movement, every decision he makes can affect the tilt of the universal plane, and his entire purpose is directed toward maintaining its balance.*

We all keep the universe in balance.

We are not robots, or lemmings marching toward the cliff. Our lives matter. Our decisions matter. True, we are governed by restrictions large and small, affected by forces visible and invisible. Yet we make choices that influence what we see and who we become. Together, we tilt the universe toward darkness and death, or life and light.

Third: *Suddenly I become aware of a multiplicity of voices inside me, speaking, singing, clamoring for attention. What I thought was one voice, me, is in fact many different characters with different qualities, like actors on a stage, each with a certain independence, yet a necessary part of the whole. Each one has a right to be heard, and once heard and known, takes its place in the internal geometry of the entity known as me. I need to understand these characters, not judge or repress them, yet not be seduced by them either, simply honor the paradoxes and contradictions of the being that I am, rough edges and smooth, pretty and not pretty, lovable and unlovable.*

The third one—I thought I'd figured it out by the time I got back to my bike and pedaled home that day. But this was not just some random insight. This was a way of life. *E pluribus unum*: out of the many, one. What makes sense for a whole nation also works for a nation of one. If I try to pick and choose which parts of me are acceptable and condemn the rest to Siberia, I would spend a lifetime at war with myself. All the players in my interior cast of characters—good, bad, and ugly—must be known, allowed to speak, and led to the baptismal waters. Maybe then the terrible schisms inside me would heal and my soul would find peace.

Seed
in ground
Does it know
Tree?

One of those dark days in my twenties, I was walking under a railroad bridge in Philadelphia near the university, and a noisy freight train lumbered overhead. A pathetic, skinny, homeless man stood nearby, looking up at the train, mouth wide open, eyes fixed on—whatever he saw, but it wasn't a freight train. And I remember thinking, *That's probably where I'm headed. That guy's my brother.* And the prospect didn't bother me. I welcomed it. The idea seemed, somehow, heroic.

Those seven little words about seeds and trees gave me comfort in the middle of the most difficult, most doubt-filled, most hopeless time of my six-plus decades on terra firma. My "dark night of the soul."

The simple question: does a seed know it will become a tree, even though it's only a seed and has done nothing but lie dormant under the earth? Asking the question, I knew the answer. No matter how far gone I was, I could feel that tree in me. The tree already existed.

Since then I've known illness, loss, betrayal, death—nothing compares with the moment when I wrote that brief poem. The accumulated weight of fear and isolation would have killed my spirit were it not for the dreams that guided me and gave me hope that what was happening had a purpose and the story would somehow end happily:

A house—my house—a fire consumes it, destroys it. Nothing left but ashes. Where the house was, a circle forms. Inside the circle, a new being grows. The circle becomes an egg. There is silence, waiting, stillness as the new life slowly congeals. Suddenly the egg becomes the earth, and a man stands on the earth. His hands are joyously outstretched to the heavens. The earth opens up and a cornucopia of people, animals, flowers, and beautiful created things pours out in a stream of life energy.

This dream came to me in 1976. A few years later the outpouring of creativity it depicted was happening. And now, I look at the life I've led and the gifts I've received and given, and I see those five dark years as like the drawing of an arrow, or the intake of breath before a shout, or the pulling back of the forearm of a boxer before the fist strikes with accuracy and purpose.

In 1976, I was a lost soul, chasing dreams further and further inside, no idea when or how I would rejoin the world and get on with the life I was given to lead. Ten years later, I had finished my education and was working seriously as a photographer. I'd run a gallery, created exhibits, written grants and raised money, and was about to launch a huge project that briefly brought Philadelphia's cultural institutions together—more than seventy-five of them, large and small—to celebrate the art of photography.

Reciting my résumé is tedious, even for me. But I look back in wonder at this life of extreme oscillations, from a desperately introverted chaser of dreams to being so involved in living that I barely had time to think a creative thought, though I never forgot what had happened, and made sure the "interior dialogue" got the necessary attention so when the quiet times came, the creative work was waiting, ready.

I look back on those decades, look at the stuff I made or helped to make, and think of the end of the dream about the burning house. My life of the past thirty-five years has been a fertile cornucopia, an outpouring of creativity that as a teenager I would not have dared to dream was possible. Eventually, when I began to recognize the underground connections between what happened to me and the Judeo-Christian mythos of death and rebirth, crucifixion and resurrection, I saw that, in my own crazy way, I had died and been "born again." I had been "saved."

The words fit, but uneasily. I had earned my "salvation" with a lot of interior suffering. Healing had happened, but completely beyond my control and as a result of processes of growth that were light-years beyond my understanding. For a while I looked for explanations and similarities and found many, from ancient Greece to Babylonia to the Psalms. Eventually I realized that my power cable fits best in the Christian outlet. I was living the Christian story long before I had the imagination to call it by its name. The events and parables from the life and death of Christ have become for me an idealized, but emotionally intense, model or template for my own journey, starting with a simple metaphor from the Gospel of John: "Except a grain of wheat fall into the ground and die, it remains alone; but if it dies, it bringeth forth much fruit" (John 12:24).

Explanations are less important now. What matters is that somehow in those hard years a spiritual discipline began to grow, a set of skills that led me to a state of interior "togetherness." What I now call prayer. You could say I found my voice as an artist. But there's more.

Creativity, the life of the spirit, my moral and empathic connections with people—for me there is no separation. All grow from the same source. The same interior friendship. The same unseen dance partner. The same dance.

Roots drink deep.
Leaves breathe air,
and light.
How long before
the fall?

God is Dream, growing and healing; contradictions, connections, complexities, simplicities, enigmas; countless other things known and unknowable, seen and felt. But I look at those words and they're just that: words signifying the character of something that has no definable form, that all logic says is a complete impossibility, and that my own skeptical voices poke holes in with the best hole-poking debunking rationalists around.

Yet I rest comfortably in my remembering, knowing that I saw what I saw, and I use the language of religion to give it a name and a framework to hang it on, but all I can really say is that I was lost and now I'm found. I was broken and now I'm healed. I participated but I did not control. The faith I had in the truth of Dream was the only thing that kept me sane.

The biggest and baddest container inside my God word box, the deepest and widest vessel that most sums up the God word but is also the most elusive and terrifying to confront, is *Truth*. God is Truth.

What is Truth? Truth is a pathway. A fierce desire. A hunger to discern, to separate the real from the unreal. To say that I want a thing, I don't have it yet but I will find it, and be found by it, and it will be solid and honest, and when it happens I will hold fast and never let it go, never let my attention be drawn from the search, never willingly accept the false and call it true when its lack of truth has been revealed—that is the core, the very essence of what I call God.

This is more than simply not telling lies. It's living a life where Truth is like a light carried inside, carried gently, barely visible, but emanating from the pores and animating the words, yet gracefully, without trying.

Now, as my body does its slow-motion demolition derby, as systems malfunction and every day I'm reminded of how little time a person has, I ponder who I was and am, and I see how close I came to screwing it all up so many times, how I stand with one foot on either side of the balance point and every day, in quiet prayer, say, *Today my God, my friend, my invisible dance partner, help me today to not turn away, help me today to discern wheat from chaff.*

Some days it's like putting my hands in my pockets and whistling; other days it's a dim light in a vast darkness; and once in a while, it's the sun rising and the clouds opening and the light pouring through.

There is no prayer I can utter that is not known already, so I begin each day simply kneeling, not literally (bad for the knees) but inside. I don't know what's true but maybe today I'll catch a glimpse and God please help me to know the truth about how I am doing, help me to see the difference between me and not-me, to separate real and not real. That is my wordless prayer. If I do that, what I need, to get done what I was given to do—it will come.

Okay, sometimes I have to dig through the dirt with bare hands like a desperate lunatic. Whatever it takes, whatever it takes.

The seed sprouted and began to grow, and whaddaya know, it's become the tree. How did that happen? I was too busy to let the how and the why distract me. I want to say thank-you, but whom do I thank? Something designated by the word G-O-D? Should I thank the supernova whose unimaginable energy forged the complex carbon molecules that are the building blocks of my life, of all life on earth? How does a grain of sand thank the infinitude of waves whose pounding created the beach? And yet I must say thank-you, because I am known and loved and remembered, even by the universe that would snuff out my puny and insignificant life in a nanosecond without mercy.

Figure that one out—no, don't bother. Waste of energy.

How long before the tree falls? Having too much fun just being here to care. But the shadows are getting longer.

The thing is, it's not really about the words. Thank-you is more like a place, inside. What matters is finding that place. Sometimes words can help me get there. But when I do, ideas like "inside/outside" and "here/there" just get in the way. All that matters is adding my drop to the river.

Seed grows, tree falls.
After that, nobody knows. Except
I'll be goin' where the river goes.
The River of Dream.

from ... to #1, 1993-94

Intimations of Immortality

Good Friday Sermon, delivered at Trinity Episcopal Church, Ambler, Pennsylvania, April 18, 2014

Today is April 18th, which means there are less than two weeks left to celebrate National Poetry Month. I did some research and discovered that April is also Mathematics Awareness Month and Financial Literacy Month. Math and money have many friends, but poetry can always use a little boost, so I'm going to begin with a few lines by the English poet William Wordsworth, from a famous poem with a long title but usually known simply as *Intimations of Immortality*:

> *There was a time when meadow, grove, and stream,*
> *The earth, and every common sight,*
> > *To me did seem*
> > *Appareled in celestial light,*
> *The glory and the freshness of a dream.*

Suppose I asked you to sum up the entire human adventure—the nature of being us—in a single word. What might it be? I heard a stand-up comic recently say that the most important thing in life is "pain management." There are days when I agree.

I like the word the great Lutheran theologian Paul Tillich often used in his sermons: *predicament*. A predicament is a problem, but more: it's a head-scratcher. A dilemma that no amount of intellectual heavy lifting can resolve. Life itself, the nature of it, its very essence, is an unsolvable problem. A predicament.

We're here tonight, in this ceremony that is at the very heart of the Christian journey, to face that predicament head-on, grab it by the scruff of the neck, maybe shake it up a bit, and see if any light comes out.

Here's the predicament as I see it. From the day we're born, we're given an incredible gift. The gift of life. We're given bodies that move and dance and sing, we're given senses that see and touch and taste the world, we're given minds that think and feel, and most importantly, we can grow. We can become more than we are—not different, but more—and as we do that, doorways open, and we're able to share with others what we've received ourselves, and we receive what others have to offer, in abundance.

But everything we're given is taken away.

I recently retired from a job of twenty-four years. If you're curious, I was a curator at an art museum. I put pictures on walls and thought deep thoughts about them. One day a bunch of us geezers who worked there were standing around gabbing, and the subjects ranged from back problems to surgeries, from Grecian Formula to cancer statistics. The conversation kept getting grimmer and grimmer and grimmer until finally, mercifully, one of the staff comedians said, "Well, so much for intelligent design!"

Every living creature is given, as a birthright, the wonder of simply being here. And we all must experience the loss of this gift. Perhaps slowly. Perhaps in the blink of an eye. We see it happening all around us, we feel it happening in our own bodies.

Okay. We're born, we die. Not much deep thinking there. So what about that predicament?

When my sister died ten years ago, I managed to nab one of her favorite objects, a small framed print of hills and farms and people working, with a quote below the picture that says, "Be glad of life, because it gives you the chance to love and work, to play and to look up at the stars."

Love, work, play—pretty basic stuff. Especially the work part—no shortage of that in our lives.

But looking up at the stars. What's that line talking about? To the poet William Wordsworth, it was meadows, groves, and streams bathed in heavenly light. To my sister, it was looking at the night sky. I wonder what "it" is for each of us. Because I'll bet everyone here has something. A memory, a feeling, a look in someone's eyes. A gentle touch barely felt, that says there's more to life than what we can see at first glance. There are secrets, mysteries. There are moments when we seem poised to touch the eternal, when the divine presence is as real as the air we breathe and the ground we walk on.

But then it's over, the feeling is gone, and it's just us, you and me, here, in this place, and a wondrous strange place it is, this earth, this life.

So let's see if I've got this straight. (A) As the bearers of life, we're all immeasurably wealthy, and we're born with the urge to explore and grow. But (B) it's all going away. And as if that's not enough, (C) there are those hints and whispers, those intimations of immortality. Like living and dying, they're also part of being human, aren't they? To look up at the stars. To see the world as Wordsworth did, like a dream of light. To look in the eyes of a newborn child, or to be there at the death of someone you love, and feel that light as a presence in the room, something you can almost taste and touch.

This, my friends, is whatcha call a predicament. We're temporary, vulnerable, mortal bits of flesh, with antennae tuned to the eternal frequencies, but the reception isn't that clear, and like a bad cell phone connection, the voice on the other end sort of blips in and out, and then there are those annoying dropped calls, and we say, *Can you hear me now, can you hear me now*?

But wait a minute—with all this talk of the unsolvable problem, the predicament, aren't we forgetting something? Just watch the crowd near the end zone at a football game, and often there's a sign waving urgently that reads, "John 3:16." God gave his only begotten son so that if you believe, you receive eternal life. It almost sounds too good to be true. I'm a Christian. In fact, I'm a baptized Episcopalian—got the paperwork to prove it—so I definitely win the prize in the Cracker Jack box, right? Sometimes you even hear it described as the "eternal reward"—like it's a gold star we get for good behavior.

The tricky part, to me, is that simple little word *believe*. I believe all kinds of things and don't even break a sweat. I believe in red lights, because I know what will happen if I don't. I believe little kids think I look like Santa Claus. But what does Jesus the Christ say are the necessary conditions, the ticket to ride, of belief? He says, Give away all you have, take up the cross, and follow.

Now I don't think he expects us all to become Mother Teresa. On the other hand, reciting the Nicene Creed once a week is probably not the sum total of what he has in mind for us either. I can only give you my own take on that word *believe*: belief means a no-holds-barred, dive in to the deep end, total commitment to the journey, to living the life—to seeking and asking and knocking on the door, without knowing exactly what you'll be finding and receiving, or if the door will even open.

The Gospels don't give us a free pass to the promised land. They invite us—no, they insist, they demand—that we follow Christ. And where does he lead us? Into the very heart of the predicament.

Follow Christ into life. Be glad of life, as my sister's wall plaque said. Live, love, work, play, grow. Find your place in the world. Figure out what you have to give, and give like there's no tomorrow. When in doubt, give it out. That's belief. That's following Jesus.

Follow Christ and be baptized into life, follow even into the very light of heavenly transfiguration, but keep going, follow all the way to those two terrifying places, Gethsemane and Golgotha. Where he fell to the ground in agony and said, "Take this cup from me." And where the eternal son of God knew what our bodies tell us every day, knew the doubt and uncertainty that everyone feels, when the connection seems to be broken, the cell phone call is dropped, and we look up to the heavens and there are no stars. Or as Jesus put it while dying on the cross, those incredible words from Psalm 22, "My God, my God, why have you forsaken me?"

Follow Christ into the heart of the predicament, into life, and into death itself. And then, follow him into eternity. Whatever that means, wherever that is. I don't claim to know. And I take with a very large grain of salt those who say they do—even the haunting and beautiful stories from people who, thanks to the hard-won knowledge of medical science, have been there, briefly, and come back. What interests me most about near-death experiences is not the heavenly reportage— the number of pearls on the Pearly Gates, or whether Saint Paul is left- or right-handed.

What intrigues me is that when those folks return, their love of life is often renewed, and they end up more committed to being here and making a difference.

Life, death, and eternity. This is the terrifying and beautiful predicament that we live out every day. There's no greater mystery. Which is why I love the Passion story. It's honest. People who don't like religion often say the Bible is a "happy drug" that helps people avoid reality. No. *You can't get much truer than the cross.*

In my own moments of doubt, when I feel broken and abandoned, when I know in my very molecules that the gift of life is slipping away, the Passion story reminds me that these are the moments when we're most human, when we're most beloved of God: when we're inside the predicament, not figuring it out but living it out. The Passion story gives me the strength to do my best to seek the path that Christ walked, seek to live as he did. With courage. With forgiveness. With generosity. Keep seeking all the way to the very end.

Jesus was always on the lookout for the honest search, and reserved some of his sharpest words for those who thought they had all the answers. It's the depth and hunger of the seeking that matter. If you seek, Jesus says, you'll find. If you ask, you'll receive. If you give the door a solid knock, eventually it will open, but probably not until you're ready to let the light shine into the darker corners of your soul. You may not be comfortable with what that light reveals. That's also part of the Passion story—looking inward, seeking the truth about ourselves, like the disciples who ignore Jesus's suffering at Gethsemane, or Peter learning what it feels like when he, not the evil Judas, becomes the betrayer.

When the disciples feel remorse for ignoring and betraying their friend, they learn something important about belief—that it doesn't have a handy escape clause that lets you opt out when the going gets rough, or maybe lets you take a little time off when belief gets in the way of something pretty that you really really want.

Belief is a connection—a living relationship—that needs to be nurtured and respected. Ignoring, denying, betraying that deep, interior friendship is pretty much the worst thing you can do, about as bad as shutting yourself off from the river of love that flows invisibly from one human heart to another.

If this sounds familiar, it should. Love God and love your neighbor as yourself. The two great commandments in the Gospels. We hear that L-word so often. It emerges from our lips so easily, so routinely. How hard can it be? From Elvis to Shakespeare to Betty Crocker puttin' some lovin' in the oven—everybody knows about love, right?

But we face difficult choices where the path is not so clear. And the decisions we make really matter. We mess up. We fail. We lose our way.

Jesus never says we're supposed to be perfect. He likes the losers, the rejects, the failures. The Bible is filled with people who make mistakes. What about that shepherd who leaves his flock of a hundred to rescue one lost sheep? From an economic point of view, there is no logic to this. Logic says, sacrifice the one to protect the many.

But who among us can claim that they've never felt abandoned, alone, hungry to be known and loved—seeking and asking, with precious little finding and receiving?

At one time or another, we're all lost sheep. Sometimes the only thing you can do is blindly walk the path where your feet have taken you, and trust that you'll hear the still, small voice of the shepherd in the distance, calling your name.

And then, somehow, we go home.

I don't know it. But I feel it. I see glimpses in the heavenly light in groves and streams, in the clear light of the stars at night, in the shining eyes of people every day. And these glimpses are part of the natural order of things, part of the predicament of life, death, and eternity—the predicament that every creature who's ever lived and ever will live knows from first breath to last.

We are all born of this earth, lost sheep who easily stray from the flock, who need the shepherd's call and a saving touch to find our way. We are no better, no worse, no higher, no lower, no more or less deserving, than any other creature who's ever lived, who's ever looked up at the night sky and wondered, "Why? Why are we here? Where are we going? Is what we can see all there is, or is there more? How was I made, the one who is here, now, doing the seeing and the asking?"

We began with poetry, so let's end the same way. An American this time—Carl Sandburg—a few lines from one of his last poems:

Long ago—as now—little men and women knew in
their bones the singing and the aching of
these stumbling questions.

Amen.

Earth Music #26, 1993–94

Home

We'd forgotten why we come to this place, but then we unlocked the front door and remembered. Just past the boardwalk, beyond the wooden pathway, farther than the green garbage can, there it was. That line, all the way left to all the way right, or right to left, who cares, doesn't matter, there it was.

The line stretched and stretched and stretched—out to the last lonely star in the farthest galaxy that had been around long enough for a few of its photons to fly a billion light-years and into my hungry eyeballs.

The next morning we woke up at dawn, when the faint orange glow had just begun to separate earth and sky. She got out her brushes, I got out the cameras. We waited. We watched, as the slow symphony of light and space unfolded, and we did our best to approximate and speculate and if possible perhaps we just might *create* something, anything that would even begin to communicate what being there, in that place, was doing to our synapses and corpuscles and microscopic arteries where the ancient nourishing waters come and go, ebb and flow.

There, there, in that place, on that beach, it happens, it shows itself, a rim of red on the horizon cloud, then the first hint of fire, until finally, oh yes, there it is, there it is. An unbroken thread of sunlight stretching halfway around the world, flowing back to the endless islands of landless algae floating in primordial seas, algae that turned and twisted and crunched up and congealed into us, you and me, vast conglomerations of cellular flesh desperately searching for water and light and air and earth and places to live and die.

Water, all the way to the sky, moving, cresting, undulating, flowing, pushed by the wind toward the shore, not a smooth mirror or a tranquil pond, it's a sea of light, all the way to the edge of the world.

I am light as a falling maple seed, heavy as the iron at the core of the earth, moving like a graceful dancer, pounding like a blacksmith's hammer.

Yet I am nothing, a tiny fleck of sand, an empty cup waiting, hoping, to be filled.

There is no name for what my eyes are seeing, no word can contain it.

The water, the light, this whole big ball of a world, thank you, thank you infinite ocean and universe without end, thank you because there is no end and no beginning, only eyes that see and hands that move and touch.

Eyes inside, and eyes outside, see all that I am, and I am. I see. I am.

Later, when it was over, I sat on the porch, watching her apply pigment to paper, while the light poured over the earth like an endless river. Suddenly my cells spoke to me, and I said the words aloud, terrifying words, but also soothing, peaceful.

"This is a good place to die."

I said it again, after a minute or two had gone by. "This is a good place to die." I worried that she'd think I might drop dead right there, on the porch of the little house by the ocean, in the sunlight, drop dead. But no, she barely looked up, barely heard the words, and I was glad she was so absorbed in approximating and speculating and creating a thing that tries to communicate the impossibility of what we were seeing, what we knew we'd see from the moment we opened the door, glanced at each other, and smiled.

My cells said, stand up, so I stood up, slowly unfolded my arms, spread them to the sky, and let the light flow over my body like baptismal water.

Yes, a nice place to die, I thought, because here, in this place, death would be like stepping over a puddle or skipping down a sidewalk. One more hop and there you are. From beauty, to beauty. As simple as that.

A good place but not a good time. Not yet.

"Time for breakfast?" She had turned toward me, saw me standing there, white beard over blue jacket over wrinkled gray sweatpants, camera dangling on shoulder, arms spread, cheeks glistening with tiny sweaty trails of water and love.

"Sure," I said, and as our eyes met, briefly, we smiled again, because we knew that home is where the light is. No need to go anywhere. Home is where the light is, and we were already there.

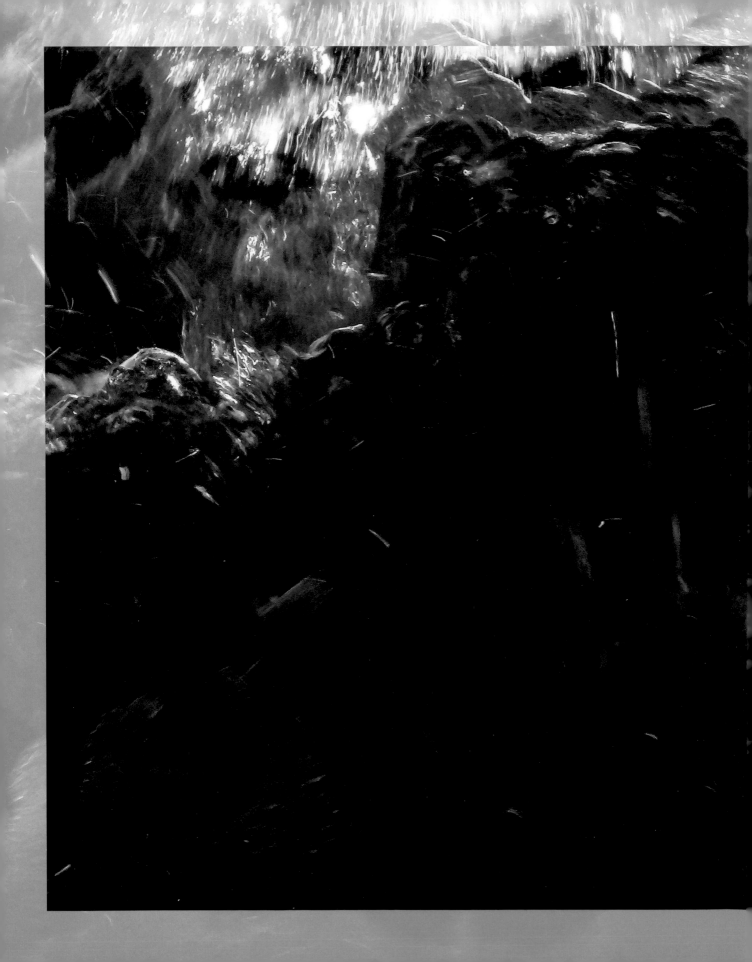

Laudate Dominum

I'm not the kind of person who tries to sniff out signs of divine purpose in a song heard while grocery shopping, or in a butterfly fluttering its wings on a nearby marigold. Having said that, I've had enough inexplicable things happen to make me doubt, seriously, that the logic of the scientific method is the only path to knowledge, and that what we can measure and weigh and hold firmly in our hands is the only reality.

There are rare, transcendent moments of "agreement"—when creative energies flow with unusual intensity and clarity—when the normal boundaries between inner and outer, self and non-self, seem to dissolve. Eyesight becomes sharper, roots sink deeper. Coincidences occur that the rational mind can observe but never adequately explain..

In my late twenties, after the long journey I've tried (and failed) to describe in these pages, I knew the moment had arrived. I had to write some music—real music—finally, my own music. Sing my song. It was a time of the greatest joy, a time of birth, when my body was alive with eros and my soul was seeking and finding beautiful connections with others and my creative energy was flowing.

I had been reading the poems of E. E. Cummings, his love poems, so lush, so lovingly, astonishingly fresh and erotic. Suddenly I had an idea—write some songs using these poems I'd fallen in love with. At that very moment, without hesitation, I grabbed my massive Cummings tome, the complete poems. I reached down and eagerly, hungrily opened the book, didn't matter where, just wanted to read some words, find a poem or two that might tell me there was gold in those clean white pages.

I expected to do a lengthy search, gradually winnowing contenders down to finalists, until the keepers finally emerged. But the first poem I turned to—when I read the first line—"the moon is hiding in her hair"—I felt continents lock together and heard warm wind flow through open windows. There was music to be written. Not tomorrow: now. I went to my piano and wrote the very notes that got the music started.

That was one of those inexplicable moments. Logic can always find a reason why. But logic is irrelevant when the magic is flowing.

It was magic. That's what it felt like, and I see no reason to call it otherwise. Magic. My interior life leapt out and poured itself into the molecules around me. I knew what I had to do. Seize the moment, make something beautiful, push it as far as it could go. So I did. And when the piece was finished a couple months later, I knew I was, in my own way, "born again," from toenail to cerebellum.

A few days ago, I fell asleep while holding my iPad. I might have been playing online Scrabble, or maybe I had a hankering for music while I worked. Instead I drifted into unconsciousness. As I woke up, I heard a sound, and when location and awareness began to return, sounds became music, and what music! A choir, an orchestra . . . deep, dark, rhythmic patterns, words in Latin, what were they singing—*Laudate Dominum*—of course—Stravinsky! *The Symphony of Psalms*, one of my favorite pieces of religious music: devout, serious, troubled, and at the end, calm, transcendent.

But where was the music coming from?

From my iPad. I glanced down and saw my fingers resting near the appropriate link. Very, very odd, since I had no memory of putting them there. Somehow, in my sleep, I found this particular spot of touch-sensitive glass. *Gosh, must be part of God's plan,* I thought. Logically, ridiculous. But why not just go with it? What's the harm? So I restarted the Stravinsky, but realized that I hadn't looked at the words in several decades. So with a modest bit of Googling, I read the words while the chorus sang. And suddenly I knew how this book needed to end.

Laudate. Gratitude and praise. Praise that-which-we-call-God-but-has no name. Praise creation in all its magnificence and mystery. Praise even those who doubt the mystery and miss the magnificence, because their doubt is itself magnificent and noble. Doubt and denial are threaded through the weave of the certainty and acceptance of the faithful. Honest believers never deny their own doubts, nor do thoughtful scientists deny the wonder and mystery of what they study.

Albert Einstein had no interest in a personal God, but he was known to admire what he called the "structures" of the universe, and he expressed wonder at the vast phenomenon he studied, even saying that the mysterious is "beautiful" and the "source of all art and science."

My father was a scientist, and a damned fine one. Yet he sat with me one day in my teens, on our back porch, and as we watched a maple seed drift down with its elegant circling motion, he turned to me. "Do you think you could design something like that?" he asked. "Sure, why not," I replied, and he just shook his head in silence.

Laudate. Praise. That's where I end this book. I don't know why the universe is so beautiful and so scary, why it does what it does and doesn't do what it doesn't. I only know that I'm moved to sing and dance and celebrate and create, shout hosanna and say, what a gas it is to be alive!

Laudate Dominum. But the Latin God-word is no better than the English—it just hits the air with more gravitas. I prefer *Laudate Omnium.* Praise all. Praise everything. I don't know how to sift out the nuggets from the pebbles and pyrite. I don't know what to praise and what not to praise. So, praise it all.

I can see the raised eyebrows, hear the shocked silence. Everything? Praise starvation and tsunami? Mass murder, disease, and despot? Even my own skeptical voice asks, *Are you crazy or just stupid?*

Probably both. But other than knowing that killing and otherwise harming people is generally a bad thing to do, I'm not smart enough to discern the tides of history or the purpose of events. I'm a sunflower inhabiting my little patch of earth, growing and blooming and dying, and that's good enough for me.

Laudate Omnium. A friend told me about a college class in which professors were asked to imagine it was their last day on earth, and invited to deliver their final lecture. Made me think about what mine would be. Maybe I'd spend the first hour getting to know the people in the audience, which would no doubt be of manageable size! We could all tell our stories—at least the executive summaries.

Then, instead of dispensing wisdom, I'd play a crude three-minute video I made of our two older grandkids, Ty and Ollie, running around in circles in the front yard of our little rental beach house, on New Year's Eve, waving sparklers and shouting for joy at the pure pleasure of bringing a little more light into the world. "Sparklers are awesome!" *Laudate Lumen! Laudate Dominum!*

Because my old friends Michael and Steve, separately, each in their own way, and gently, have helped me feel the deep ambivalence they have at the word *Christ*, and how much suffering their Jewish brothers and sisters have experienced over the centuries at the hands of those who claim their authority from the very Gospels I've come to love—and really because who said it better than the Psalmists anyway—I'd end my lecture by reading some of the words that Stravinsky cobbled together for his Symphony of Psalms. Maybe I'd get my wife to read them, because she's a poet and has the theater in her blood:

I waited patiently for the Lord: and He inclined unto me, and heard my calling. He brought me also out of the horrible pit, out of the mire and clay: and set my feet upon the rock, and ordered my goings. And He hath put a new song in my mouth: even a thanksgiving unto our God. Many shall see it and rejoice, and shall put their trust in the Lord.

—Psalm 40

Praise ye the Lord. Praise God in his sanctuary: praise him in the firmament of his power. Praise him with the sound of the trumpet: praise him with the psaltery and harp. Praise him with the timbrel and dance: praise him with stringed instruments and organs. Praise him upon the loud cymbals: praise him upon the high sounding cymbals. Let everything that hath breath praise the Lord.

—Psalm 150

Then I'd say what I say to you, faithful reader. *Laudate.* Praise. And thanks for sharing an oar with me for a while.

Time to row my boat homeward. Thank you, friend. Praise all, and thank you.

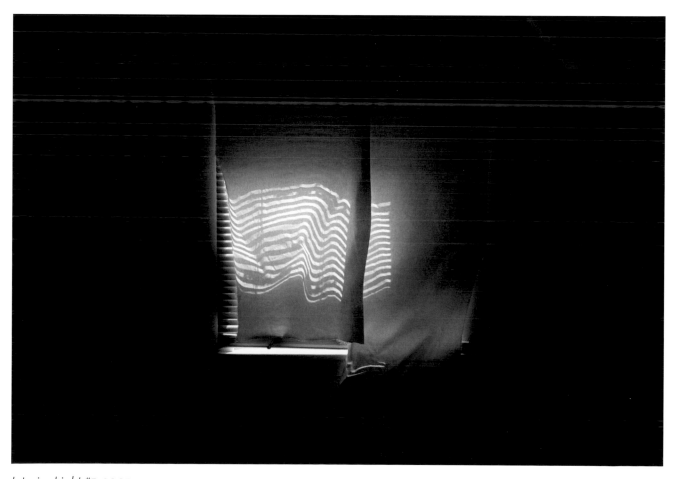

Interior Light #5, 2003

Acknowledgments

Gee whiz, that's a weak word. Four syllables, too—you'd think it would have more, you know, oomph to it. I guess I could dig up a Latin phrase that sounds all nice and Latiny, but the old-fashioned "thank you" my mother recommended gets the job done. Thanks, Mom.

So I say thank-you to my Helen, my wife. Talk about deserving a medal. Wow. I have not been easy to live with, writing a book while we sold our house and found another and got rid of or stored or moved all our stuff. And throw in a couple of surgeries. A gold medal.

I thank my brother Jim, his wife Betty, for their steadfast love—my sister Wendy for her courageous love—and my parents, who've taken their lumps at my hands, but in my dotage I see the bigger picture, and OMG, they were beautiful, beautiful souls. I know, technically that's twice for Mom in the thanks department. Whatever. Being married to one for a couple of decades, I've learned that the "mom" job is not for sissies.

This is weird, but I want to thank the people, both strangers and friends, who've disagreed with me, who even at times have openly struggled against both me and what I care about. Opposition clarifies the eyesight. And sometimes leads to unexpected and rewarding friendship.

My editor, Paula Brisco. Knows my moves better than I do, and gives all she has to make it good. Thanks, Paula!

My gallerist, friend, supporter, co-conspirator, and fellow warrior Santa Bannon, and her husband Tom Shillea—generous spirits, my gratitude.

My designer, Sherilyn Kulesh, who did more than design—she read, she took chances, she understood. Forever grateful.

My friends who absorbed and commented: Jamie, Mark, Ron, and especially Alex, whose priesthood of the soul has nourished me for nearly four decades.

Finally, I simply say, thank you. Again. Thank you.

"Not all those who wander are lost."

–J. R. R. Tolkien